# THE CLASSICS IN TRANSLATION

# The Classics in Translation

AN ANNOTATED GUIDE TO THE BEST
TRANSLATIONS OF THE GREEK
AND LATIN CLASSICS
INTO ENGLISH

BY

## F. SEYMOUR SMITH

Deputy Librarian, Hornsey
Honorary Editor, "The Library Assistant"

WITH A PREFACE BY

### HENRY BARTLETT VAN HOESEN

Associate Librarian, Brown University

## CHARLES SCRIBNER'S SONS
LONDON     NEW YORK
1930

THE WORK WHICH FOLLOWS IS PART OF A
THESIS ACCEPTED IN 1928 BY THE LIBRARY
ASSOCIATION FOR THE HONOURS DIPLOMA
IN LIBRARIANSHIP

# PREFACE

For the full appreciation of a piece of literature one must, of course, understand its particular language medium and its literary form as well as its atmosphere or historical setting and its thought content.

But a variety of studies and reading interests which even our fathers hardly dreamt of have crowded Latin and Greek, Alcaic strophes and hendecasyllables, out of the curricula of an increasing number of students, and the college graduate who "took" Latin and Greek has loved and lost. He does a great deal of serious and delightful reading (let us hope) in an ever wider range of interests—but little Latin and Greek.

To students who have missed their Latin and Greek, the way is made easy, by translations, to read the "record of the best thoughts" (as Emerson defined literature) which, though not the whole of literature, is the essential element which justifies its existence. And the reader who once studied the classics may, in translations, refresh and enlarge his acquaintance with the thought-content of classical literature, and may also recollect, may recapture the charm of Homer or Horace.

Even to the student who reads Greek with fair facility, good translations have something to offer. I shall always be grateful to the one Greek professor who actually put a translation into my hands—Jebb's "Sophocles". I would translate a few lines for myself and then read Jebb—and Jebb was somewhat better! Reading the Greek and the English thus concurrently may not have improved my Greek vocabulary and syntax but it did wonders for my literary appreciation.

Furthermore, literature is not only literature, it is also documentary, source material, political history, economic history; history of all sorts uses literary texts as sources. Even the mediaeval universal histories and encyclopædias are not too bulky for the enterprise of historians who, by translating, make available to their students an amount and variety of source material which could not otherwise be covered in the "course".

No student, classical or non-classical, should be allowed to finish his literary or historical training without having the field of reading in translation opened up to him as Mr. Seymour Smith does it in this book, or as an historian, a classics instructor or a "Reader's adviser" might do it, supplementing Mr. Seymour Smith's book with comments from his own experience.

HENRY BARTLETT VAN HOESEN

BROWN UNIVERSITY

# CONTENTS

PART ONE

## THE THEORY OF TRANSLATION

PART TWO

## TRANSLATIONS FROM THE GREEK

PART THREE

## TRANSLATIONS FROM THE LATIN

# LIST OF ABBREVIATIONS USED

| | |
|---|---|
| b. . . . . . | born |
| Bibliog. . . . . | Bibliography |
| Bohn's Class. Lib. . . | Bohn's Classical Library |
| Bohn's Eccles. Lib. . . | Bohn's Ecclesiastical Library |
| Broadway Trans. . . | Broadway Translations Series |
| c. . . . . . | *circa* |
| C.U.P. . . . . | Cambridge University Press |
| Cal. . . . . . | California |
| Camb. Ency. Co., N.Y. . | Cambridge Encyclopædia Company, New York. |
| Camb. Hist. Eng. Lit. . | Cambridge History of English Literature. |
| Class. . . . . | Classical |
| Class. Rev. . . . | Classical Review |
| Comm. . . . . | Commentary |
| Conn. . . . . | Connecticut |
| Cont. . . . . | Continued |
| d. . . . . . | died |
| D.N.B. . . . . | Dictionary of National Biography |
| E.E.T.S. . . . . | Early English Text Society |
| Edit. . . . . | Edited |
| Edn. . . . . | Edition |
| Fl. . . . . . | Floruit |
| Ind. . . . . | Indianapolis |
| Intro. . . . | Introduction |
| Lit. . . . . | Literature |
| Loeb Class. Lib. . | Loeb Classical Library |
| New Univ. Lib. . | New Universal Library |
| N.Y. . . . . . | New York |
| O.U.P. . . . . | Oxford University Press |
| p., pp. . . . | Page, pages |
| Pr. . . . . | Press |

| | |
|---|---|
| Pref. . . . . . | Preface |
| Publ. Co. . . . . | Publishing Company |
| Repr. . . . . | Reprinted |
| Soc. . . . . . | Society |
| S.P.C.K. . . . | Society for the Propagation of Christian Knowledge |
| Times Lit. Sup. . . | Times Literary Supplement |
| Trans. . . . . | Translated |
| Univ. . . . . | University |
| Univ. Tut. Pr. . . . | University Tutorial Press |
| Vt. . . . . . | Vermont (U.S.A.) |
| Vol. . . . . . | Volume |

# INTRODUCTION

So far as can be ascertained, there exists no other bibliographical guide giving the information the present work is designed to give. Moss's well-known "Manual of Classical Bibliography", for instance, was intended to be a guide for collectors rather than for readers of the classics. Consequently it is a bibliography in the strict sense of the term, and gives not only nearly all of the translations into English up to 1800, but also a good selection of translations into other European languages. In addition the author gives a valuable list of the finest texts. This book, apart from the fact that it is over a century old and therefore both out of date and difficult to obtain, is emphatically not one which is easily used by the general public. It is not evaluative and its information is important mainly to the bibliophile and the bibliographer.

J. B. Mayor's "Guide to the Choice of Classical Books" is now out of date, and in any case is not very useful as a guide to translations, since its chief aim was to record the best texts. The lists of translations which are included are very meagre and are not annotated. Again, Mr. F. M. K. Foster's "English Translations from the Greek" is a useful book, but its compiler's aim was merely to list the translations without annotation or selection: it is therefore useful only as a bibliography.

The best guide extant is the little pamphlet published by the Oxford Press, and entitled the "Claim of Antiquity". This is very useful and authoritative, but the authors included in the lists are confined strictly to the most important, such as Homer, Sophocles,

Aristophanes, etc. Moreover, the notes are somewhat exiguous.

There are a few other notable books, some of which, like Schweiger's "Handbuch der classischen Bibliographie" (Leipzig, 1832), are similar to Moss's work; German, however, being the chief and English the subsidiary language in the sections dealing with translations. Others, of which Hoffman's "Bibliographisches Lexicon der gesammten Litteratur der Griechen" (1838) and a French bibliography by Paul Masqueray ("Bibliographie pratique de la littérature grecque", 1914) are the chief, are very useful, but only as mines of bibliographical information.

Far from being easy to obtain, therefore, guidance to the best and most notable translations of the classics is so scattered that most inquirers have to rely on the recommendation of a teacher, a librarian or a well-read friend. These in their turn are restricted to the books which they themselves have read or read about. So far as librarians are concerned, the books they have read about form a very large class, and in a lifetime they accumulate a wonderful and reliable store of information. These human bibliographies, however, come into contact only with a very small percentage of the world's readers, so that, in the main, many students are obliged to "trust to luck" when they select a translation to read or to study.

This desk-book, then, is an endeavour to give concisely the information necessary to those who desire to read good English translations of works originally written in Greek or Latin. The information at present exists in hundreds of books, essays and articles, and is practically unavailable without the arduous

As a "notable" translation, however, it perhaps takes precedence of every other book in the whole of this bibliography; it is therefore followed by short quotations from Charles Lamb, Professor Saintsbury, Charles Whibley and Frederic Harrison, which together express the weakness and strength of this famous version. Thus, by consulting this bibliography, the reader will be in a position to buy or read Chapman's Homer with his eyes open. He will know that he has not read Homer when he has read Chapman; his own taste and imagination, prompted maybe by the infectious enthusiasm of Professor Saintsbury or Charles Whibley (to whose full-length criticisms he will fly if he is leisured and wise), will tell him that he has read an English epic as great as any in the language. On reading through the full list of translations, he will find, set out for his intelligent choice, all the other outstanding versions of Homer. The librarian can thus take a rapid survey of Homeric translation, which may aid him in selection and recommendation; the teacher and the student will be able to select the version which fulfils their personal requirements. Under this particular heading, of course, the range is wide, extending from the literal prose version of Lang, Leaf and Myers to the poetical version of Worsley.

Use of the asterisk and double asterisk has been made where necessary, so that a rapid selection may be facilitated.

It will be noticed that some few versions have been included which are decidedly not regarded at the present time as good and reliable. A striking example is Potter's translation of Aeschylus. The reason for the inclusion of such translations is that they are still popular and are often reprinted in standard editions. The annotations given reveal their limitations, so that the student is not likely to be misled. In the case of Potter's Aeschylus the annotation is quoted from Boswell's "Johnson", for the Doctor's blunt estimate of his contemporary's work is now regarded as a just one.

Only the best of the *Bohn's Classical Library* have been included, as this wonderful series was very unequal in merit. In those cases when the Bohn translation is the only one yet published, it has been recorded on the principle that any translation is better than none. Because of their special value all of the volumes belonging to the *Loeb Classical Library* are listed, sometimes with critical estimates taken from reliable reviews. In range, scholarship and textual accuracy this series is undoubtedly surpassing all others. It is very expensive, however, for the ordinary purchaser, most of the authors represented occupying more than one volume. Josephus, for instance, will take eight volumes, thus making the total cost of this author £4 ($20).[1] Furthermore, nearly all the poets in this series have been presented in prose versions, which in the eyes of most readers is a serious loss; and, finally, most of the translations are new. This makes it imperative that every student should approach his author with his eyes open. If he would read Plutarch as a magnificently vivid presentment of character and history, then he must read him in North's translation; if he must have Plutarch, and Plutarch only, he will not be disappointed with Professor Perrin's version in the *Loeb Library*. In every case a decision must be made

[1] One must not forget, however, that the parallel text and translation amount to two books in one.

with a view to the special requirements and temperament of the reader. The object of this guide is to make
this decision a simple matter.

Any system of evaluation of such a vast body of
literature must have its drawbacks, and the compiler is
fully aware that it may be objected that the critical
annotations appended to many of these works may
reveal the personal bias of the critic. This is true; but
nevertheless the opinion of the trained reviewer, who
is into the bargain nearly always a classical scholar of
some distinction, is surely the best guide to the value
of a translation that is at present conceivable. No one
man could adequately evaluate all of the works listed
in this bibliography, but it is claimed with some confi-
dence that the quotations from learned reviews and
authors, aided by the personal opinions collected over
a considerable period from cultured readers, do express
to a great extent the general opinion of the works.
The compiler would here like to express his grati-
tude for the great help he has received from many
friends, and in particular for the assistance rendered
by his wife.

Undoubtedly the only way (for those unable to read
the original) to become closely acquainted with a great
classic is to read it in several translations. Chapman
retains Homer's grandeur and dignity, but loses some
of his swift beauty; Pope has rendered his swiftness
but has made him well-mannered and monotonously
precise; Worsley has made him sing sweetly enough
in beautiful Spenserian stanza, but he has lost his
grandeur; Cowper, alas, is often dull; Derby is worth
reading; so, too, is Butler's amusing version; while
not to have read Butcher, Lang, Leaf and Myers is

to have neglected the best prose version. Each member of this noble group of scholars has some excellence denied the others. To know them all is to know Homer as well as he can be known to those who have no Greek. In this way only can we unlock the door which leads to that antique garden of heroic exploits wherein so many have found delight.

# PART ONE

# THE THEORY OF TRANSLATION

# CHAPTER ONE

# FROM THE TUDOR TRANSLATORS TO POPE'S HOMER

*Such a hard thing it is to bring matter*
*out of any one language into another.*
THOMAS WILSON (1570)

Professors of literature can describe great epics and great lyrics, but for their creation they can give no recipe; nor can they express a magic formula for the making of a perfect translation from one tongue into another. Translations, like epics, when they are works of genius give to us with one hand the right to talk of standards and rules whilst with the other they take that right away—or at least rob it of its value by magnificently disregarding all rules when it suits their purpose. Most great writers, in fact, make a new set of rules for lesser men every time they bring to light a new creation.

Curiously enough, the English writer who has surely broken less rules than any other great poet is the one who has best expressed this freedom of genius:

> If, where the rules not far enough extend
> (Since rules were made but to promote their end)
> Some lucky license answer to the full,
> Th' extent proposed, that license is a rule.[1]

Even in this age of Public Health, no human child is so much weighed, measured, tested and sounded as are the literary progeny of great writers. The tragedy, the epic, the novel, the lyric and most of the other

[1] Pope, "Essay on Criticism".

literary forms have been defined, analysed and commented on, almost from the moment of their first appearance; yet until the eighteenth century little notice was taken of the subsidiary art of translation. With the exception of Dryden's essays, nothing of importance was written on the subject until Pope translated Homer; and until the end of the nineteenth century the only book written directly on translation seems to have been Tytler's "Principles of Translation" (1791). Many translators, however, have explained their own particular theories in the shape of prefaces to their works.

Of these prefaces there are thousands, and after reading the most important the impression is received that each translator, sensible of the fact that the perfect translation does not exist, had come to the conclusion that the best thing to do was to set forth his credentials for the task he had undertaken, to explain his method of working, to compare this with some other author's (usually Chapman's, Dryden's or Pope's), and then to throw himself on the mercy of the "general public". He is often very humble, and forestalls the deadly charges of dullness, inaccuracy, unfaithfulness to his text, incongruity, over-literalness and presumptuous ineptitude which contemporary Bentleys are wont to hurl at scholars' heads, by stating that he has done his best with a hopeless task, that *he* cannot hope to succeed where so-and-so has failed, and that, after all, everything not perfect is a compromise. He indicates with a savage gesture the text of Horace, and asks if it can be expected that he should be able to re-create that perfection without loss; he defiantly mutters of the incommunicable rhythm of Pindar, the burning passion

[ 24 ]

of Sappho, or the swift dignity of Homer, and makes us sadly realise that to render simultaneously their form, accents and thought in a new language is indeed an almost impossible task.

Nevertheless, nearly one hundred translators have attempted the impossible with one author alone, and have given us English versions of Horace, some of which are faithful to their original in one respect and others in another.

The early translators did not trouble to be faithful to their texts. Like Aelfric, they merely wished "to be clear and readable above all",[1] and many later writers have echoed his words in different forms.

It would seem that Thomas Wilson's naïve admission which heads this chapter found no echo in the hearts of most of the Tudor translators, for they translated with that impetuous vigour and ease which nearly all the original writers of that period possessed. Like Drake, these literary adventurers voyaged into seas uncharted and unknown, and singed the beards of the great with reckless audacity. They did not so much succeed in "bringing the matter of their authors from one language into another" (although this was indeed their main object) as in "composing a new masterpiece on an ancient theme" or in giving us "a set of variations on ancient motives".[2]

Such lack of scholarship will not serve now, even though it be wedded to the splendid prose which many of the early translators wrote. They have, it is true, left us a heritage of English writing which must always inspire and sometimes awe; they have succeeded in

[1] Aelfric's Preface to his "Homilies".
[2] See Whibley's articles on the Tudor translators in Vol. 4 of the "Cambridge History of English Literature".

[ 25 ]

writing books which live as original works; but all have been, or will be, superseded as translators in the modern sense of the word.

This being so, it is obvious that there is little to be learnt from them on the art of translation as a matter of conscientious scholarship combined with adequate power of expression in English. As the Tudor age was one of glorious prose, we should perhaps be thankful that their comparative lack of scholarship left these early translators free to express their own ideas and genius in their own way. We demand and can have accurate scholarship now, but who among our translators can write prose comparable to North's? We may have to read the *Loeb* Plutarch for its admirable faithfulness to the Greek, but when the master's back is turned we slyly draw North from our desks to read, not always Plutarch, it is true, but something which at times is even better. Here is not only a translation, but also a classic of English prose. Fortunately for English letters, Sir Thomas, instead of following the *theory* of his illustrious predecessor, followed his practice. "For", says Amyot, "the office of a fit translator consisteth not only in the faithful expressing of his author's meaning, but also in a certain resembling and shadowing forth of the form of his style and manner of speaking".[1] It has been pointed out that both Amyot and North gave as much of themselves as they did of Plutarch, for which we can only be sufficiently grateful when we compare their versions with Langhorne's or Dryden's.

[1] "Je prie les lecteurs de vouloir considerer que l'office d'un propre traducteur ne gist pas seulement à rendre fidelement la sentence de son autheur, mais aussi à representer aucunement et à adombrer la forme du style et maniere de parler d'iceluy." (*Preface* "*Pericles et Fabius Maximus*".)

It is sometimes stated that the seventeenth-century translators revolted against that fidelity to text which produces strictly literal renderings; but they can hardly be said to have revolted against something which did not exist: it would be more accurate to say that the idea of literal translations was disliked and avoided. Ben Jonson, as we shall see, was later taken by Dryden as a typical literal translator, but though he had many supporters the tendency of the age was rather to follow the advice of Horace, who, by writing in "Ars Poetica":

> nec verbo verbum curabis reddere fidus
> interpres—

gave to the Tudor translators all the encouragement they needed.

Sir John Harington, the translator of Ariosto (1591), was certainly on the side of Horace, and so too was Chapman. The latter, in his introduction to Homer (1616), lays about him vigorously, seeking to justify his departures from the text:

> Alwaies conceiuing how pedanticall and absurd an affectation it is in the interpretation of any Author (much more of Homer) to turn him word for word, when (according to Horace and other best lawgiuers to translators) it is the part of euery knowing and iudiciall interpreter, not to follow the number and order of words, but the materiall things themselues. . . .

Much the same argument was used by him in the poetical preface which follows:

> . . . all so much apply
> Their paines and cunnings word for word to render
> Their patient Authors, when they may as well
> Make fish with fowle, camels with whales engender.

Yet there is a great difference between Chapman's free rendering, and the loose paraphrase which became popular in the middle of the century. In France, Nicolas D'Ablancourt was the influential exponent of these loose ideas of translation which probably had some effect on Cowley's theories. D'Ablancourt was candidly opposed to treating the original work with any respect; for his principle was to use the matter contained in the works of foreign authors for the purpose of composing what was virtually a new work on the same subject. Instead of wishing to introduce unlettered Frenchmen to the literary glories of other tongues, he simply wished to add another work to the literature of France.

This patriotic outlook, with its severe limitations, was characteristic of the age. In England Cowley, whether from the same reasons or not, produced the same kind of translation as D'Ablancourt's. Cowley may perhaps be forgiven the freedom which he took with Pindar, not because of the greatness of his "Pindarique Odes", but because of the difficulty of his task. Many a translator has come to his conclusion that "if a man should undertake to translate Pindar word for word, it would be thought that one madman had translated another".[1] Cowley's few remarks on translation are candid and clear; and since the following admission aptly expresses the attitude of his period to the art, it deserves quotation and special notice: "I have in these two odes of Pindar's taken, left out, and added what I pleased; nor make it so much my aim to let the reader know precisely what he spoke, as what was his way and manner of speaking".[2] Roscommon,

[1] Preface to "Pindarique Odes" (1647).    [2] Ibid.

Cowley's contemporary, and the almost-forgotten author of the line "choose an author as you choose a friend", was not quite so free and easy as this. He neatly expresses his advice in his "Essay on translated verse", "'Tis so much safer to leave out than add."

With the proverbial precision which rightly belonged to the next century, he shows himself to be well aware of the dangers of too much latitude. He advises would-be translators that the art is no easy one, and even goes so far as to instruct them that they should "take pains the genuine meaning to explore". "Express" is the word a modern scholar would use, although it may perhaps be granted that this was the real meaning of the injunction, but a rhyme being required for "oar", the author had no choice (in the seventeenth century) but to submit to the tyranny of the heroic couplet.

The greatest translator of this century was without doubt John Dryden. He also has left us critical remarks on translation, and they form some of the most important writings we have on the subject. He was the first critic to differentiate between the various kinds of translation, which, in his strong and logical prose, he divides under three headings: "First, that of metaphrase, or turning an author word by word, and line by line, from one language into another".[1] This kind is now, of course, known as literal translation, and as an example Dryden quotes Ben Jonson's version of the "Ars Poetica" of Horace. In our own time many of the translations in *Bohn's Classical Library* may perhaps be instanced as specimens of the same kind, which well reveal the limitations and dullness of the method. "The second way", he continues, "is that of paraphrase,

[1] Preface to "The Translations of Ovid's Epistles" (1680).

or translation with latitude, where the author is kept in view by the translator, so as never to be lost, but his words are not so strictly followed as his sense; and that too is admitted to be amplified, but not altered".[1] His example of this kind is Waller's translation of the fourth book of Virgil; a more modern example is Professor Gilbert Murray's versions of Euripides. Indeed, most of the great poetical translations come under this heading, since the great poetry of any language is such an exquisite combination of thought, words, sounds and subtle connotations that to alter a single syllable is often to bring the whole magic creation crashing to the ground in ruins. The third division, in which Dryden would have placed FitzGerald's "Omar Kháyyám" had he read it, "is that of imitation, where the translator (if now he has not lost that name) assumes the liberty not only to vary from the words and sense, but to forsake them both as he sees occasion; and, taking only some general hints from the original, to run division on the groundwork, as he pleases". The best example of this class is Cowley's "Pindarique Odes".

This is clearly and concisely put, but Dryden does not here consider the possibility of a more vague and indefinite kind of translation, with which we of the twentieth century are so familiar that, strictly speaking, we do not consider any other kind to be a true translation. This class lies between Dryden's first and second divisions, possessing the good points of both, yet remaining different from either. The modern translator, as exemplified by most of the *Loeb* scholars, endeavours to render the meaning of his author and

[1] Preface to "The Translations of Ovid's Epistles" (1680).

nothing but his meaning, in a style which is as near as possible to that of the original. Here no amplification of the text, even without alteration, if that be really possible, is allowed. To envisage the difference between Dryden's "paraphrase" and a modern translation, contrast the difference between North's Plutarch and Professor Perrin's in the *Loeb Classical Library*. In the one is often found more of North than Plutarch; in the other, a strict eye has been kept on the text, so that little of the original author is lost, while the English reads plainly and easily, almost as if it were an original work. From the following accounts of Coriolanus's arrival in Antium much can be learned:

It was evening, and many met him, but no man knew him. He proceeded, therefore, to the house of Tullus, and slipping in unawares, took his seat at the hearth in silence, covered his head, and remained there motionless. The people of the house were amazed, and did not venture to raise him up, for his mien and his silence gave him a certain dignity; but they told Tullus, who was at supper, what a strange thing had happened. Tullus rose from table and came to him, and asked him who he was, and why he was come. At this, then, Marcius uncovered his head, and after a slight pause said: "If thou dost not yet recognize me, Tullus, but disbelievest thine eyes, I must be my own accuser". (128 *words. From the Loeb version by Prof. Perrin.*)

It was even twilight when he entered the city of Antium, and many people met him in the streets, but no man knew him. So he went directly to Tullus Aufidius' house, and when he came thither, he got him up straight to the chimney hearth, and sat him down, and spake not a word to any man, his face all muffled over. They of the house, spying him, wondered what he should be, and yet they durst not bid him rise. For ill-favouredly muffled and disguised as he was, yet there appeared a certain majesty in his countenance, and in his silence; whereupon they went to Tullus, who was at supper, to tell him of the strange disguising of this

[ 31 ]

man. Tullus rose presently from the board, and, coming towards him, asked him what he was, and wherefore he came. Then Martius unmuffled himself; and after he had paused awhile, making no answer, said to him "If thou knowest me not yet, Tullus, and, seeing me, dost not perhaps believe me to be the man I am indeed, I must of necessity bewray myself to be that I am". (194 *words. From North's version,* 1579.)

It is clear from these two quotations that, while far from being what we should call a paraphrase of Plutarch, North's version does answer admirably to Dryden's definition of a paraphrase. The Elizabethan version is immeasurably superior to the modern, and its superiority lies in this, that North never scrupled to add to his author, provided that by doing so he could change a bare recital to a dramatic and vivid picture.

Consider the opening: Prof. Perrin translates the plain statement that many people met Coriolanus; North, with the imagination of the born writer, senses the lack of vividness at once; he therefore boldly inserts "when he entered the city of Antium, and many people met him in the streets". By the simple insertion of the scene of action a dramatic change has taken place in the narrative. By comparison the original is abstract and lacking in colour, while in North's translation the reader is given a living picture of a crowded city with a single figure in isolation.

To achieve his effect North takes half as many words again as Professor Perrin, which gives some idea of his insertions. Again, in Perrin, Coriolanus covers his head, in North he muffles his face. The gain is striking and needs no comment. "They of the house, spying him" is frankly added, and here again we feel the thrill that

[ 32 ]

only the greatest writers can give. In the twentieth century North would be inaccurate; in his own time he was merely doing what every other translator did.

The inaccuracy of the sixteenth and seventeenth centuries is now no longer tolerated, however, unless it be wedded to English of such unique quality that the criticism of the schoolmaster is lost amid the approval of the literary public, and these occasions are rare indeed. The Tudor age was an age of great translations because it was an age of great prose; the present period is the golden age of accurate translation. Very rarely do we have the good fortune to light on a work which, like FitzGerald's "Omar Kháyyám", "is much too good to be a good translation".

Yet, although Dryden in the preface to his Ovid does not mention the "modern" manner of translating, he must have had a similar method in his mind; for in the preface to his Virgil he declares his intention is "to steer betwixt the two extremes of paraphrase and literal translation, to keep as near my author as I could, without losing all his graces". Most critics think he steered badly, and went disastrously near the rock of paraphrase. He lost Virgil's graces when he put in his own, which are, of course, of no mean order. Yet Dryden's graces, pleasant as they may be, are not Virgil's and so are out of place in a translation of the "Aeneid" which endeavours to keep as near to Virgil as possible. Continuing his intentions, Dryden says that he had endeavoured to make Virgil speak such English as he would have spoken if he had been born in England at that time. It is this effort which probably upset the steering; unless indeed he wrote the preface after he had finished the epic, and in this case, the preface is in the nature of a justification for what he must have known were very decided lapses from his text. This objective, admirable as it seems in theory, leads to such freedom that most writers now rule it out as misleading. In the first place it is impossible to determine how Virgil would write were he at Oxford to-day; and the result of trying to do so is mere guess-work. Most people would guess that he would write like Tennyson, yet how different is that poet's style from that of Dryden! There is doubtless some truth in the saying that each age should produce its own version of Virgil and Homer, but it is unwise to insist on the use of current idiom, as the translation of the Bible into twentieth-century English has shown. Some such idea as Dryden's was in the minds of the Tudor translators, but we read their works as originals not as translations. Moreover, by the adoption of this method much of the historical value of a classical author's work would be lost, and so, too, would be one of the chief values of translation—the understanding of the ages which produced the ancient classics. Translators *qua* translators are of an age, not for all time; each generation wishes to express itself anew; yet the aim of the modern writer is not so much to make Virgil and Homer speak like English poets of to-day as to produce a translation which shall eclipse all others, and to do for the poets what many critics used to think Jowett had done for Plato.

When we turn to Dryden's Ovid, however, we find that he is condemned by his own words as an imitator. For the translator, says he, has "to consider, at the same time, the thought of his author, and his words, and to find out the counterpart of each in another language;

and besides this, he is to confine himself to the compass of numbers, and the slavery of rhyme". This, he continues in his sturdy way, is like dancing on a tight-rope with fettered legs. Consequently "I take imitation of an author to be an endeavour of a later poet to write like one who has written before him on the same subject; that is, not to translate his words, or be confined to his sense, but only to set him as a pattern, and to write as he supposes that author would have done had he lived in our age, and in our country". He goes on to point out the dangers of this method of translating in any other hands than Cowley's! He condemns imitation and verbal version in no uncertain language —"Imitation and verbal version are . . . the two extremes which ought to be avoided . . . the sense of an author, generally speaking, is to be sacred and inviolable".[1] When he came to translate Virgil, however, this last dictum was forgotten. Modern translators also find that when they approach the poetry of an ancient language it is almost impossible to steer a course between those two extremes.

Alexander Pope, the translator of the other great classical epic, was theoretically entirely in agreement with Dryden. In his interesting preface to the "Iliad", he states that it is "the first grand duty of an interpreter to give his author entire and unmaimed", and lays it down that the translator must follow his original in tone and diction; that where the original is lofty the translator must follow its flights; but that where it is plain and lowly so too must the translator be plain in transferring the meaning. But Pope, like Dryden, found the task too much for him. If we compare the

[1] Preface to "Ovid's Epistles" (1680).

following typical passages we shall see how near to his own ideal he kept:

> The Prince replies: "Ah! cease, divinely fair,
> Nor add reproaches to the wounds I bear;
> This day the foe prevail'd by Pallas' power:
> We yet may vanquish in a happier hour:
> There want not gods to favour us above;
> But let the business of our life be love:
> These softer moments let delights employ,
> And kind embraces snatch the hasty joy". . . .
> Thus having spoke, the enamoured Phrygian boy
> Rush'd to the bed, impatient for the joy.
> Him Helen follow'd slow with bashful charms,
> And clasp'd the blooming hero in her arms.
> *Pope's "Iliad", Bk. III., 1. 440.*

He answered: "Pray thee, woman, cease, to chide and grieve me
> thus,
Disgraces will not last. Look on their end. On us
Will other gods, at other times, let fall the victor's wreath,
As on him Pallas put it now. Shall our loves sink beneath
The hate of fortune? In love's fire, let all hates vanish, come!"
. . . With this he went before,
She after to the odorous bed.

> *Chapman's "Iliad".*

Then Paris made answer, and spake to her, saying: "Chide not my heart, lady, with hard words of reviling. For the present hath Menelaus vanquished me with Athene's aid, but another time shall I vanquish him; on our side too there be gods. But come, let us take our joy, couched together in love." He spake, and led the way to the couch, and with him followed his wife.
> *A. T. Murray's version in the Loeb Classical Library.*

Pope's version reads smoothly enough and conveys the story with a certain dignity. But in place of Chapman's simple and dignified "Pray thee, woman, cease", we are given "Ah! cease, divinely fair"—conveying a quite different nuance from most other versions. Then the saccharine embraces snatching the "hasty joy" and the last four lines with their inevitable epithets give again a quite different impression of Homer from most other versions. "Him Helen followed slow with bashful charms" is a line of which any poet might be proud, but it is neither like Homer nor, from what others have told us of her, does it give a passable portrait of Helen. Anything more unlike a "bashful" maiden than Helen would be hard to think of—that much discussed lady may have been many things she should not have been, but she never earned *this* epithet.

It thus seems that a great poet like Pope found it impossible to give his author "entire and unmaimed", that he was forced to use frequently his own "tone and diction" and not Homer's, and that, in short, he found his own precepts impossible to follow consistently.

# CHAPTER TWO

# FROM TYTLER'S "PRINCIPLES" TO PHILLIMORE AND POSTGATE

AT this point it will be convenient to consider the only treatise written in the eighteenth century on the art of translation by one who was not himself a translator. "The Principles of Translation" was written by a man who confined his literary activities to history and criticism. Alexander Fraser Tytler, later Lord Woodhouselee, published his famous essay in 1791.

Surveying translation and translations as an amateur, Tytler had some advantage over his predecessors, for he had no axe to grind, and so could consider his subject with calm detachment.

Briefly put, a good translation according to the result of his researches should satisfy the following canons:

(1) The translation should give a complete transcript of the ideas of the original work.

(2) The style and manner of writing should be of the same character as that of the original.

(3) The translation should have all the ease of original composition.

A translation may be described as good, he says, when "the merit of the original work is so completely transfused into another language as to be as distinctly apprehended, as strongly felt, by a native of the country to which that language belongs, as it is by he who speaks the language of the original work". To this most people will readily agree; the difficulty being to decide exactly how a native of the country to which the language of the original belongs does apprehend and feel the work, The man who is so steeped in the literary genius and spirit of two countries and languages that he can accurately determine and re-express shades of meaning, accents and associations with the subtle skill needed to satisfy this requirement is rare indeed—as rare as a good translation.

In stating the case so precisely, however, Tytler did point the way to an ideal, and since his views were not associated with any particular translator or work their general application is valuable in a way in which Dryden's and Pope's were not. Tytler, of course, was thinking of translation from any tongue, but the ancient classic languages present special difficulties. The exact shades of meaning and the associations of certain words in particular phrases are almost certainly lost to us. The word "love", for example, is so often used in our daily speech that we know instinctively what we mean by it; it is only when we have to define such words in our vocabulary that we realize how vaguely we understand their meaning, and how elusive are their limitations. The word itself affects us in a special way which is the psychological result of our manner of living, our temperament and experience. When we read the "Symposium" the word "love" seems to have other meanings than those we know of, so that we strongly desire to break down the barriers between modern life and ancient Greek life and custom which seem to separate us from those hidden meanings. The difficulty is almost insurmountable in poetry, where words are greatly intensified in meaning and association.

With Tytler's first proposition nobody can disagree, for any work which fails to give a "complete transcript of the ideas" cannot rightly be termed a translation. The second condition laid down seems to condemn definitely prose renderings of poetry, since no one can assert with truth that "the style and manner of writing" of a prose "Aeneid" is of the same character as that of the original. Yet when translating poetry it is obvious that the best way to keep Tytler's first rule is to make a prose version. Chapman, Dryden and Pope have all shown how impossible it is to render great poetry by great poetry without distorting the ideas of the original work. This point is important when considering nineteenth-century work, since in that period the prose version of a poetic original became very popular. Tytler's third requirement is absolutely essential to any work if it is ever to emerge from the study and the schoolroom into the outside world. It is in this respect that many otherwise good translations fail: for it is undoubtedly this quality which is so rare when combined with accurate scholarship. By reason of the strength of his original talent a great writer, when he essays translation, often finds it impossible to prevent his own style and personality from overshadowing or modifying his author's. His attempts to give his renderings the ease of original composition more often than not succeed so well that little trace of the native work remains.

In this connection J. H. Frere, the author of one of the two classic renderings of Aristophanes, says that the language of translation "ought, as far as possible, to be a fine, impalpable and invisible element, the medium of thought and feeling and nothing more; it ought never to attract attention to itself. . . ."[1] It will readily be seen that when a poet of Pope's genius sets himself the task of translating Homer, there must

[1] "Quarterly Review", vol. xxiii (July 1820).

inevitably be a struggle between the two creative minds. The eighteenth century is often called the "classical century" but the classicism of Pope and his school was poles apart from the spirit of ancient Greece. Intellectually, the romantic poets, from Shelley to Keats and Byron, were much more sympathetic to Athenian ideals than were the poets of the eighteenth century. Pope's language is not only "the medium of Homer's thought and feeling" but is also a vehicle for his own self-expression.

No future translator of Homer can afford to neglect Matthew Arnold's famous essay, first published in 1865. Arnold often writes like a schoolmaster, but it cannot be denied that in his essay on "Translating Homer" he lays his finger on those qualities in that author which must be preserved in any adequate translation. In the most important part of his essay he deals with fidelity to the original, and details his considered opinion on the best metre for English renderings of Homer. He recommends the English hexameter, and is therefore inclined to be hard on Cowper. "To suppose", says he, "that it is fidelity to an original to give its matter, unless you at the same time give its manner: or rather, to suppose that you can really give its matter at all, unless you can give its manner, is just the mistake of our Pre-Raphaelite school of painters. . . ." It would appear from this, that Arnold would have little sympathy with the characteristic translations of our own age—the prose translations of a poetic original.

It will be convenient here, before considering the more recent translations, to give some attention to the theories expounded by some of the best translators of this generation and that preceding it. Numerically,

[ 41 ]

the work of translation overshadows even the most crowded age that has been considered—the Tudor age.

Benjamin Jowett has become an Oxford legend; his monumental translation of Plato has become an English classic: his opinions on translation are therefore of importance. Jowett was first amongst translators to insist on the necessity for satisfying both "the scholar and the unlearned reader" in one and the same translation. He would have translations "idiomatic and interesting". Further, he improved on Dryden's rule, that the translation should impress the reader as the original impressed the author's contemporaries, by affirming that the true translator should "seek to produce on his reader an impression similar or nearly similar to that produced by the original", i.e. by the original on the modern reader.[1] This distinction is very important, for it answers the chief objection to Dryden's ruling. Finer still was Jowett's belief that "the feeling should be more important than the exact words". "The excellence of a translation", he continues, "will consist, nor merely in the faithful rendering of words, or in the composition of a sentence only, or yet of a single paragraph, but in the colour and style of the whole work".[2] The main point of disagreement between Jowett and most modern critics is that he recommends and defends the practice of altering and modifying faulty and obscure passages.

Although the practice of "improving" an author is sometimes sensible, it so often proves dangerous that it cannot be unreservedly recommended, and therefore is best condemned. It is better for translators to give us their authors unaltered and in entirety, be the faults

[1] Preface to Jowett's "Plato", 5 vols. O.U.P.      [2] Ibid.

and obscurities what they may. How else can an impression similar or nearly similar to that produced by the original be conveyed? Faults to some are merits to others:

> Those oft are stratagems which errors seem,
> Nor is it Homer nods, but we that dream.

The office of a translator is to translate, not to improve. It may have been very lazy of Plato to nod, but the passage of the centuries has hallowed his rest; not even the great Jowett should try to awaken him. All we can hope is that by this time a delighted intelligentsia in Elysium have had the pleasure of hearing a lively dialogue between Plato and Jowett, in which the late Master of Balliol has been utterly refuted and unmercifully taken to task in the true Socratic manner. Maybe Boswell has transferred his allegiance, in which case the dialogue will have become a heavenly delight.

One of the most successful translators of his time was D. G. Rossetti, to whom every lover of poetry is indebted for his perfect translation of Villon's "Ballade des Dames du Temps jadis". Here indeed is a translation which gives the lie to the assertion that perfect transference of form, style and content is impossible in the same work. Many of Rossetti's translations are almost unique, in that they conform to his own theoretic ideal without losing their original qualities. "The life-blood of rhythmical translation is this commandment—that a good poem shall not be turned into a bad one. The only true motive for putting poetry into a fresh language must be to endow a fresh nation as far as possible with one more possession of beauty".[1] When

Preface to "Dante and his Circle" (1861).

paraphrase is the only means of fulfilling this purpose, he thinks, paraphrase the translator must. When he translated Villon's poem, however, a comparison with the original will show that little is lost, nothing added, yet the original beauty is retained.

A very interesting theory is put forth by Walter Headlam in his "Book of Greek Verse". In Headlam's opinion, unless there already exist in the translator's language a native form and style corresponding to that of the original, then translation with great success is not possible. It is this belief which explains for him the fact that we have as yet no adequate translation of Homer, nor anything more than a passable rendering of Pindar. Until some great English writer creates a great English epic in Homeric form and manner the necessary inspiration and spade-work to prepare the way for an English poet to re-translate the "Iliad" will be lacking.

This theory is certainly supported if a parallel is accepted between Aeschylus and Shakespeare, Sophocles and Milton. We have good translations of both of these two ancient dramatists, and by this theory the reason is to be found in the fact that two native writers have already perfected styles which are akin to those of the Greek writers. Certainly Swinburne's rhythms and metres introduced a Greek quality into English verse which has greatly influenced the renderings of Euripides made by Professor Gilbert Murray. Swinburne's pagan soul was so near to the Greek spirit that his "Atalanta in Calydon" reads like a Greek play; indeed a fine scholar recommends it as being a better example of a Greek play than any translation. Jowett's monumental version of Plato, says Headlam, was made possible by Ruskin's prose. Jf this be so, and few refute it, perhaps there is some justice in the late J. S. Phillimore's surprising condemnation of that work. Ruskin's characteristic style certainly seems much too complicated and heavy-laden for the bright, keen-witted and nimble Plato, with his playful irony and his flashing rapier of question and attack.

Mr. Phillimore, in the preface to his translation of Propertius, agrees with Jowett in one important point at least, for he states therein that he designed his translation both for the scholar and for the ignorant reader. This he thinks an unfortunate necessity. Faithfulness to text he deems to be all-important, yet he dislikes the prose rendering of poetry. "How shall prose render poetry and yet remain prose?" he asks. To this question may be added, And how shall prose render poetry and yet create a real translation? To these questions no direct answer can be given; everything depends on the extent to which the inevitable sacrifices are made. Something must be altered, therefore something must be lost. It is only the genius who can achieve that delicacy of touch which alone will happily render the masterpiece of another mind without spoiling it.

"To translate one language into another", says Phillimore, "may be compared to executing a painter's theme in sculpture. To translate from verse in one language to prose in another is like the attempt to render a painter's effect in some medium which discards one of the original artist's resources; like an engraver who tries to interpret a coloured painting in black and white."

The second analogy is apt and illuminating, but the

[ 45 ]

first seems faulty, because of the incongruity of the example chosen. The comparison is surely unsound, for colour is a totally different medium from stone, while Latin and English cannot be strictly termed totally different mediums, as they are both capable of achieving the same effects by the same means. The sculptor, on the other hand, sets out to express a quite different emotion from the painter. In sculpture there is no equivalent whatever to the medium of colour, by which the painter produces his illusions of actuality.

Since he is a practising translator, we may take it that Mr. Phillimore does not view the problem quite so pessimistically as would appear from his essay. Unlike Jowett, he would be faithful to his author to the extent of being absurd in his translation if his original is absurd. He would even reproduce a mixed metaphor. The same scholar has also presented some of his views in the form of a pamphlet, "Some Thoughts on Translation". This, together with Mr. Postgate's volume on translation and Mr. Heitland's small volume, "A Few Words on Translation", are the most important pronouncements made in recent years on the subject.

In Phillimore's pamphlet there is an echo of the idea already noticed in Mr. Headlam's preface—that of the effect of previous literary work in a certain genre, on the translator of works which come within the same class. It is Phillimore's opinion, too, that at certain periods in the history of a language that language is ripe for certain translations. For the germ of this theory he refers the reader to Brunetière's "Développement des Genres", a work of the greatest importance in the history of criticism. Another of his most important points is that the translation should be in the same key as the original; this being allied possibly to Tytler's second rule, where it will be found that "he only is perfectly accomplished for the duty of a translator who possesses a genius akin to that of the original author". At the same time, Phillimore argues forcibly for the supremacy "of the rights of English" in an English translation. He rightly maintains that somehow or other the translator must render his author adequately, and yet manage to produce a piece of English which can be read with pleasure, "not merely as a curiosity but as a piece of English".

When we consider Mr. Postgate's volume of theory and practice, entitled "Translation and Translations", we find that there are here strong indications that the art of translation has now become more or less stabilized. In this volume the author not only shows that he is in agreement with many of the older rulings but that he can also, as a practical translator, prove those rulings to be correct and reliable.

> By general consent, though not by universal practice, the prime merit is faithfulness, and he is the best translator whose work is nearest to his original. . . . The faithful translator will give the letter where possible, but in any case the spirit.

In the course of his analysis, which in importance, scope, force and accuracy challenges comparison with Dryden's, Mr. Postgate maintains that while "version" necessarily involves change or turning, "translation is transference". By literal translation we are to understand a translation which is the nearest intelligible rendering of the words of the original, whether the expression would have been employed in the circumstances by a native writer or not. Translations must be idiomatic if they are to be read. In opposition again to Jowett, Mr. Postgate thinks that the translator has no right to avoid repetition which is not avoided in the original; nor must he be incongruous and talk of the Devil in Catullus. After an essay which on the whole is the best exposition we have of modern theories, the author concludes with a definition of his ideal translator: a master of both the languages with which he has to deal—a practical master of his own and a critical master of the foreign tongue.

In the foregoing pages an attempt has been made to present a brief critical sketch of most of the important theories which have governed the art of translation from the Authorized Version of the Bible to the present day. Our Chapmans, Drydens and Popes will continue to write of strict theories and ideals in prefaces, but they will continue to forget them in practice; and the scholar who is not an original genius will still continue to give us new translations of the classics.

Moreover, we happily still have in our literature that same spirit of classical imitation (as distinguished from translation) which gave the seventeenth-century lyric its unique delicacy and charm. The works of Rochester, Herrick and Suckling all testify to the great influence of the Greek Anthology and of the amatory poems of Catullus and Anacreon. Sometimes the only link with Greece and Rome is an allusion to a pretty story, a happy paraphrase of an apt simile or merely the faint flavour of an antique phrase. Faint though the echo may be, something of the light grace of Anacreon and Catullus was added to English literature during the Restoration. In these instances of mere imitation or allusion, the writer has no theories or rules to hinder him and can allow his art and his learning to join hands and take him where they will: his sole aim is self-expression and he dips into the classics only as a privileged pilferer. Like Fielding, he considers "the ancients" to be merely "a rich common, where every person who hath the smallest tenement in Parnassus hath a free right to fatten his muse". His justification for this attitude, if justification be needed, is that in using the classics thus he has not only often added to the glory of his own literature but has sometimes even succeeded in adding to the works he has absorbed and used again.

But the true translator has a more difficult, if less original, task; for he must rigidly repress all desire for personal expression, and bend his art to the fullest expression possible of his author's thought.

The modern translator realizes, with Calverley, that he has two main duties to consider—his duty towards his original and his duty towards his readers. The great translator is he who can fulfil both duties fairly, without undue favour to either side.

A summary of the main rules now governing translation may be submitted thus:

(i) That the ideas in the original composition must be rendered without omission or addition.

(ii) They must also be rendered in a style and manner as near as possible in their general effect to the style and manner of the original.

(iii) That as far as may be considered consistent with the foregoing, such liberty may be allowed as will enable the translator to present a work which may be read with all the ease of an original composition.

When the work in question is in prose the finest translators of to-day conform to these ideals. It is only when the translation of poetry is considered that the greatest difficulties of transference are encountered. The *Loeb* translators seem to have argued that if the ideas in an original poem are to be rendered without omission or addition, then that rendering must be in prose. They are probably correct in their judgment. But what becomes, then, of the style and manner of the original? In most cases it will be found that scarcely any trace remains.

The translator of a work of prose has this great advantage over him who would render poetry: that the medium of prose is in general less likely to have those rare and almost inexpressible qualities which make the poet's song a thing apart.

The travesties which the French call translations of Shakespeare can make us realize what we must be missing when we read Racine or Virgil in English. The subtle beauty of

> Sunt lacrimae rerum, et mentem mortalia tangunt

may be divined even by one ignorant of the full meaning, but how shall its meaning and beauty be fully transposed into another language without loss? We shall be lucky if we find we can render its meaning in English without obscuring "that sense which was bright and pure"; but the task of reproducing the music of the original without disturbing the meaning is one which might daunt the greatest of poets. In English, for instance, lines such as:

> And dying put on the weeds of Dominic
> And in Franciscan think to pass disguised

are not to be transmuted or disturbed without loss. The poet's thought has hardened as in a mould and the music of his words must either be left untouched or lost for ever. "A great author", said Cardinal Newman, "takes his native language, masters it, partly throws himself into it, partly moulds and adapts it, pours out his multitude of ideas through the variously ramified and delicately minute channels of expression which he has found or framed." It follows, then, that the greater the author the greater is the need for his works to be translated, but, melancholy fact, the greater is the task of translation.

In general, a short poem admits of happier translation than a long one. The crystal beauty of a lyric may awaken magic phrases in another poet's mind—and the miracle happens: it is then that translations like Rossetti's of Villon are born. Here is almost perfect transference; phrase has begotten phrase; the mould has been re-cast and, rare miracle, the beauty of the original retained.

# PART TWO

# TRANSLATIONS FROM THE GREEK

# ACHILLES TATIUS

(Fl. Middle of 5th cent. A.D.)

BURTON (WILLIAM) The Loves of Clitophon and Leucippe. Trans. from the Greek by W. B. (1597.) Repr. for the first time from a copy now unique. Edited by S. Gaselee and H. F. B. Brett-Smith. Blackwell, 1923.

> The translator was the brother of the author of "The Anatomy of Melancholy". It is thought that the book was publicly burnt by archiepiscopal order. It is an interesting example of Elizabethan prose.

*GASELEE (S.) Cleitophon and Leucippe. *Loeb Class. Lib.* Heineman, 1917. (N.Y., Putnam.)

> "Smooth and agreeable throughout."—*Class. Rev., Vol.* 32, *p.* 132.

SMITH (ROWLAND) The Loves of Clitopho and Leucippe. Trans. with notes. *Bohn's Class. Lib.* Bell, 1882.

> Included in a volume which contains also the Greek romances of Heliodorus and of Longus.

# ACTS OF AUGUSTUS

*See* Res Gestae divi Augustae (Appendix).

# AELIAN

(Claudius Aelianus "Sophista". Fl. A.D. 250)

BINGHAM (JOHN) The Tactics; or, The Art of embattailing an army. 2 parts. London, 1616 and 1669.

[ 55 ]

FLEMING (ABRAHAM) A Registre of hystories . . . etc. Delivered in Englishe (as well, according to the truth of the Greek text, as of the Latine). London, 1576.

STANLEY (THOMAS) Various histories. London, 1677.

## AENEAS TACTICUS

(Fl. middle of 4th cent. B.C.)

ILLINOIS GREEK CLUB. Works. Trans. for the first time into English. *Loeb Class. Lib.*, Heinemann, 1923. (N.Y., Putnam.)

> The works of Asclepiodotus and Onasander are also included in this volume.

## AESCHINES

(Aeschines Rhetor, 389–314 B.C.)

*ADAMS (C. D.) Speeches. *Loeb. Class. Lib.*, Heinemann, 1919. (N.Y., Putnam.)

LELAND (THOMAS) Oration on the crown. London, 1771.

PORTAL (ANDREW) Oration against Ctesiphon; and, Demosthenes de Corona: literally translated. Oxford, 1755. Revised 1814.

# AESCHYLUS

## (525–456 B.C.)

*Two or more plays:—*

BLACKIE (J. S.) Lyrical dramas. (1850.) Repr. in the
*Everyman's Series*. Dent, 1906. (N.Y., Dutton.

> May still be read with pleasure. Carlyle thought highly
> of it: "spirited and lively to a high degree", he wrote;
> while Leigh Hunt, writing to the author, said, "Your
> version is right, masculine, and Aeschylean, strong,
> musical, conscious of the atmosphere of mystery and
> terror which it breathes in".

CAMPBELL (LEWIS) Plays. (1890.) Repr. in *World's
Classics*. O.U.P., 1906.

> Generally considered to be a fair but not exceptionally
> good translation. The verse runs smoothly enough, but
> compared with better translations something of the
> grandeur of the original is lacking.

*COOKSON (G. M.) Four plays: the Suppliant Maidens;
the Persians; the Seven against Thebes; Prometheus Bound. Blackwell, 1922.

*—— The Agamemnon; Eumenides; Choephoroi.
Chapman and Hall, 1924.

> By common consent an extremely fine verse translation.
> "Among the translators Mr. Cookson takes first place
> for his extraordinarily fine and vigorous rendering of
> the great trilogy of Aeschylus. It is Elizabethan in tone,
> and he sometimes uses Elizabethan freedom with the
> text."—*Vernon Rendell, London Mercury, Vol. xi, p.* 333.

\*HEADLAM (WALTER and C. E. S.) Plays: a prose translation. *Bohn's Class. Lib.* Bell, 1909. (N.Y., Harcourt.)

> "We have the seven tragedies in prose which is accurate, scholarly and dignified."—*J. F. Dobson, The Year's Work in Class. Studies,* 1910.

\*\*MORSHEAD (E. D. A.) The House of Atreus: being the Agamemnon; Libation Bearers; and the Furies. Macmillan, 1904. (N.Y., Macmillan.)

—— The Suppliant Maidens; the Persians; The Seven against Thebes; and Prometheus Bound. Macmillan, 1908. (N.Y., Macmillan.)

> A very good rendering—perhaps the best verse translation of the complete plays. "Of all the translations of the 'Agamemnon', I prefer that of Mr. E. D. A. Morshead, which seems to me by its union of accurate version with poetic vigour to stand in the front rank of English verse translation."—*Frederic Harrison, The Choice of Books.*

MURRAY (GILBERT) The Agamemnon; Libation Bearers; Eumenides. Allen and Unwin, 1920 to 1925. (N.Y., O.U.P.)

> "His style has all its usual charm, and we particularly admire the renderings of the great choral odes. . . . Though we cannot suggest a better style, it seems to us that the present version lacks something of the solemnity of the original."—*The Year's Work in Class. Studies,* 1920

PLUMPTRE (EDWARD HAYES) The Tragedies: a new verse translation with a biographical essay and an appendix of rhymed choral odes. (1858.) Repr. Isbister, 1901. (Boston, Heath.)

> "Plumptre's complete versions of Aeschylus and Sophocles . . . are the only means by which the English reader is

enabled to appreciate the delicate gradations of metre in the dramatic scenes."—*R. G. Moulton, The Ancient Classical Drama.* This estimate was written in 1898, and although it is no longer true to say that Plumptre is the only translator to render adequately the seven tragedies, yet his translations are still considered eminent.

POTTER (R.) The Tragedies: trans. into verse. (1777.) Repr. in the *New Universal Library.* Routledge, 1886. (N.Y., Dutton.)

> "*Garrick* (to Harris): 'Pray, Sir, have you read Potter's Aeschylus?' *Harris*: 'Yes: and I think it pretty.' *Garrick* (to Johnson): 'And what think you, Sir, of it?' *Johnson*: 'I thought what I read of it *verbiage*; but upon Mr. Harris's recommendation I will read a play; (to Mr. Harris): Don't prescribe two.' "—*Boswell's Life of Johnson, chap.* 37. Harsh words, but if Potter's is compared with better versions most readers will agree with Dr. Johnson.

*SMYTH (H. WEIR) The Plays: a prose translation. 2 vols. *Loeb Class. Lib.* Heinemann, 1922. (N.Y., Putnam.)

SWANWICK (ANNA) The Dramas: a verse translation. *Bohn's Class. Lib.* Bell, 1881. (N.Y., Harcourt.)

> "Miss Swanwick's beautiful translation has been published with Flaxman's designs."—*Frederic Harrison, The Choice of Books.*

TREVELYAN (R. C.) Agamemnon; Libation Bearers; the Furies: a verse translation. Bowes and Bowes, 1923. (Boston, Small.)

TUCKER (T. G.) The Choephoroi; and the Seven Against Thebes. C.U.P., 1901. (N.Y., Macmillan.)

> "If Mr. Tucker's renderings are often incorrect they are nearly always good and vigorous English."—*W. Headlam, Class. Rev., Vol.* 16, *p.* 353.

—— The Suppliants. Macmillan, 1889.

WAY (A. S.) The Seven Against Thebes; and The Persians: a verse translation. Macmillan, 1906. (N.Y., Macmillan.)

—— Prometheus Bound; and The Suppliant Maidens: a verse translation. Macmillan, 1907. (N.Y., Macmillan.)

### *The Agamemnon*

BROWNING (ROBERT) The Agamemnon: transcribed into English verse. Smith Elder, 1877. (Repr. in all collected editions of Browning's works.)

> "The work of a poet and a scholar, but its uncouthness is not the rugged majesty of Aeschylus."—*Frederic Harrison, The Choice of Books.*
> "Translated by Browning far more roughly—not to say grotesquely—in style than it deserves, but with the Greek spirit in no small measure retained."—*T. G. Tucker, The Foreign Debt of English Literature.*

CONINGTON (J.) The Agamemnon: a verse translation. O.U.P., 1907.

FITZGERALD (EDWARD) The Agamemnon: trans. into English verse. (1876.) Repr. in "Collected works".

Quaritch, 1887. (Ind., Bobbs; and Woodstock, Vt., Elm Tree Press.)

> This "version or perversion", although at times very far from the Greek, is done with such spirit and beauty that it has exacted tribute both from general readers and from scholars, although to the latter the liberties taken with the text are rightly abhorrent.

*GOODWIN (W. W.) The Agamemnon; text and trans. (Boston, Ginn, 1906.)

*HEADLAM (WALTER) The Agamemnon: a verse trans. with text, intro., and notes. C.U.P., 1911. (N.Y., Macmillan.)

> "The English translation (in verse) is magnificent, and sometimes—e.g. in the choral ode—it is sublime. It is perhaps unique in preserving the atmosphere of the original. The notes are beyond praise."—*W. H. Duke, The Year's Work in Class. Studies,* 1911.

*VERRALL (A. W.) Agamemnon; with intro., comm., and a prose translation. Macmillan, 1889. (N.Y., Macmillan.)

> This is thought to be the best prose version of the play. "This edition, whether its main thesis and its interpretations be right or not, must always remain a landmark in the history of Aeschylean criticism."—*J. N. Powell, Class. Rev., Vol.* 18.

### Prometheus Bound

BEVAN (E. R.) Prometheus Bound: a verse translation. D. Nutt, 1902.

> "An excellent translation."—*J. S. Phillimore.*

BROWNING (E. BARRETT) Prometheus Bound: a verse translation. (1833.) Repr. O.U.P. edition of works, etc.

> "She has left an inaccurate indeed, but most spirited and eloquent version of the 'Prometheus Bound'."— *J. Churton Collins.*

★CASE (J.) Prometheus Bound; Greek text with a trans. into English verse. *Temple Dramatists.* Dent, 1905. (N.Y., Dutton.)

★WHITELAW (R.) Prometheus Bound: a verse translation. O.U.P., 1907.

> SUMMARY.—For their combination of faithfulness and vigour the complete translations of G. M. Cookson and E. D. A. Morshead are to be strongly recommended to the general reader.


# AESOP

## (Fl. 570 B.C.)

CAXTON (WILLIAM) Here begynneth the book of the sybtyl Historie and Fables of Esope. . . . Trans. out of the French into Englysshe, 1484. Repr., edited by J. Jacobs, D. Nutt, 1898.

★EVERYMAN'S LIBRARY. Fables: an anthology. Dent, 1913. (N.Y., Dutton.)

> *Contents:*—Fables from Caxton's Aesop, 1484; from Thomas James's Aesop, 1848; Fables from Aesop, Phaedrus, etc., by Sir R. L'Estrange.

JAMES (THOMAS) The Fables of Aesop. Murray, 1848.

*JONES (V. S. VERNON) Fables of Aesop; with an Intro. by G. K. Chesterton. Heinemann, 1912. (N.Y., Doubleday.)

**L'ESTRANGE (SIR ROGER) Fables. London. (1669.) Repr. Golden Cockerel Press (Limited edition) 1927.

> A Selection from this translation was published in 1899 (both in England and in the U.S.A.) by John Lane under the title of "One Hundred Fables of Aesop from the English version of Sir Roger L'Estrange". Another, published by Hodder and Stoughton in 1909, is called " The Fables of Aesop, chiefly from the translation of Sir Roger L'Estrange", while still another was published in 1929 by Benn.
>
> "He [that is, L'Estrange] did his work of translation with the utmost thoroughness. . . . His chiefest qualification for the task was his mastery of his own language. . . . The work by which he is best remembered, and by which he best deserves to be remembered, is his version of Aesop's Fables. . . . His Aesop, stripped of its 'reflexions', still remains the best we have."—*Charles Whibley, Camb. Hist. Eng. Lit., Vol. 9.*
>
> "Though not literal they are eminently readable."—*Sir S. Lee, D.N.B.*

OGILBY (JOHN) Fables, paraphrased in verse. London, 1651. Repr. in 2 vols., 1672.

> Highly praised in its time, but not important now.

TOWNSEND (G. F.) Three hundred and fifty Aesop's Fables: literally translated. Routledge, 1867. Repr. 1894.

# AGAPETUS

### (Fl. A.D. 527)

PAYNELL (THOMAS) The Preceptes teaching a prynce of noble Estate his duetie. London, 1550.

# AGATHIAS

Poetic fragments. *See* Greek Anthology (Appendix).

# ALCAEUS

### (Fl. end of 7th cent. B.C.)

EASBY-SMITH (J. S.) The Songs; memoir and text; with literal and verse translation and notes. (Washington, Lowdermiek, 1901.)

EDMONDS (J. M.) Poems: a prose translation. In "Lyra Graeca". *Loeb Class. Lib.* Heinemann, 1920. (N.Y., Putnam.)

> *See* also Greek Anthology (Appendix).

# ALCINOUS

### ("Probably lived under the Caesars.")

STANLEY (THOMAS) An introduction to Platonic philosophy. London, 1687.

> This translation is contained in Stanley's "History of Philosophy".

# ALCIPHRON
(Fl. A.D. 180)

MONROE (THOMAS) and WILLIAM BELOE. Epistles.
London, 1794.

*WRIGHT (F. A.) Letters from country and town, of
fishermen, farmers, parasites, and courtesans.
*Broadway Trans.* Routledge, 1923. (N.Y., Dutton.)

# ALCMAN
(Fl. 671–631 B.C.)
*See* "Lyra Graeca", and Howe and Harrer (Appendix).

# AMMIANUS
(Fl. c. A.D. 117)
Poetic fragments. *See* Greek Anthology (Appendix).

# ANACREON
(6th cent. B.C.)
ALDINGTON (RICHARD) Greek Songs in the manner of
Anacreon. Egoist Pr., 1919.

COWLEY (A.), J. WOOD, OLDHAM and F. WILLIS.
Poems. Oxford, 1683.

> In 1923 the Nonesuch Press published a limited edition
> of "Anacreon done into English . . . by Abraham Cowley
> and S.B.", with copperplate engravings. The Chaucer
> Head Press of New York issued the copies for the U.S.A.
> The O.U.P. have also published a complete Cowley (1927).

*EDMONDS (J. M.) Odes: trans. into prose. In "Lyra
Graeca". *Loeb. Class. Lib.* Heinemann, 1920.
(N.Y., Putnam.)

FAWKES (FRANCIS) The Works of Anacreon, Sappho,
etc., trans. by a Gentleman of Cambridge. London,
1760.

> Fawkes was considered by his contemporaries the best
> translator since the days of Pope, and Dr. Johnson gave
> it as his opinion that Fawkes had translated Anacreon
> "very finely". His version is included in Chalmers's
> "British Poets".

*MOORE (THOMAS) Odes. London. 1800. (Tenth
Edition, 1820.) (N.Y., Macmillan, 1903.)

> "Elegant, spirited and highly poetical version."—*Lowndes's
> Bibliographer's Manual.* Moore's versions may still be
> read with quiet pleasure, and are to be found in most
> of the numerous editions of his poems.

**STANLEY (THOMAS) Odes. London, 1651. Repr.,
edited by A. H. Bullen, 1893. (Cheap edition,
Lawrence and Bullen, 1906.)

> "Stanley's classical scholarship was of a high order. His
> translation of Anacreon satisfies almost every require-
> ment. It is as agreeable reading as the version of Thomas
> Moore and adheres far more closely to the original."—
> *Sir S. Lee, D.N.B.*

# ANDREWES, LANCELOT

*See* Latin Section.

# ANDRONICUS RHODIUS
### (Fl. 58 B.C.)

BRIDGEMAN (W.) Paraphrase on the Nicomachean Ethics of Aristotle. London, 1807.


# ANTIPATER OF SIDON
### (Fl. 150 –127 B.C.)

*See* Greek Anthology (Appendix).


# ANTIPATER OF THESSALONICA
### (Fl. 10 B.C.–A.D. 38)

*See* Greek Anthology (Appendix).


# ANYTE OF TEGEA
### (3rd cent. B.C.)

ALDINGTON (RICHARD) Poems. *Poets' Trans. Series.* Egoist Press, 1919. (N.Y., Knopf, 1921, under the inclusive title of "Medallions in Clay".)
*See also* Greek Anthology (Appendix).


# APOLLODORUS
### (Fl. 140 B.C.)

EDMONDS (J. M.) Poetic fragments: a prose translation. In "Lyra Graeca". *Loeb. Class. Lib.* Heinemann, 1920. (N.Y., Putnam.)

FRAZER (SIR J. G.) The Library. 2 vols. *Loeb. Class. Lib.* Heinemann, 1921. (N.Y., Putnam.)

# APOLLONIUS PERGAEUS

## (Fl. 250–220 B.C.)

BURROW (REUBEN) A Restitution of the geometrical treatise on inclinations. London, 1779.

\*HEATH (SIR T. L.) The Treatise on conic sections. C.U.P., 1896. (N.Y., Macmillan.)

LAWSON (JOHN) The Two books concerning tangencies. Camb., 1764.

> "In this work Lawson has proved himself an able geometrician and a faithful translator."—*Lowndes's Bibliographer's Manual*.


# APOLLONIUS RHODIUS

## (Fl. 222–181 B.C.)

COLERIDGE (E. P.) The Argonautica: a prose translation. Bell, 1889. (N.Y., Harcourt.)

FAWKES (FRANCIS) The Argonautica in 4 books: trans. into English verse. London, 1780. Repr. in Anderson's "Poets of Great Britain", Vol. XIII, 1793, and in Chalmers's "English Poets", Vol. 20, 1810.

SETON (R. C.) The Argonautica: a prose translation. *Loeb. Class. Lib.* Heinemann, 1921. (N.Y., Putnam.)

*WAY (A. S.) The Argonautica: a verse translation. *Temple Classics*. Dent, 1901. (N.Y., Dutton.)

> This is probably the best translation. "A masterly rendering. His language savours sufficiently of the archaic and learned; his verse is varied. . . ."—*The Athenæum*, 1901.

## APOLLONIUS OF TYANA
### (4 B.C.–A.D. 96)

CONYBEARE (F. C.) Epistles. *Loeb. Class. Lib.* Heinemann, 1912. (N.Y., Putnam.)

> This translation is included in vol. 2 of Conybeare's translation of Philostratus's "Life of Apollonius of Tyana".

## APPIAN
### (Fl. A.D. 98–160)

BENECKE (E. F.) The Civil Wars. Book I. Oxford, 1894.

DAVIES (JOHN) History of the Roman Wars. London, 1679.

*WHITE (HORACE) Roman History. 2 vols. *Bohn's Class. Lib.* Bell, 1899. Repr. *Loeb. Class. Lib.* Heinemann, 1913. (N.Y., Putnam.)

> "Straightforward, clear, readable and accurate."—*Class. Rev.*

## ARATUS
### (Fl. 270 B.C.)

LAMB (J.) Phaenomena and Diosemeia: a verse translation. *Bohn's Class. Lib.* Bell, 1848.

MAIR (G. R.) Phaenomena: a prose translation. *Loeb. Class. Lib.* Heinemann, 1921. (N.Y., Putnam.)

> Included in the volume which also contains the works of Callimachus and Lycophron.

POSTE (EDWARD) The Skies and weather: forecasts of Aratus. Macmillan, 1880.

# ARCHIAS

### (B. 120 B.C.)

Poetic fragments. *See* Greek Anthology (Appendix).

# ARCHILOCHUS

### (Fl. 7th cent. B.C.)

*See* Howe and Harrer (Appendix).

# ARCHIMEDES

### (287–212 B.C.)

ANDERSON (G.) Arenarius. Trans. with notes and illustrations; to which is added The Dissertation of Christopher Clavius on the same subject from the Latin. London, 1784.

> "A masterly translation."—*Lowndes's Bibliographer's Manual.*

*HEATH (SIR THOMAS L.) Works. Edited with intro. C.U.P., 1897. (N.Y., Macmillan.)

ROBINSON (L. G.) Geometrical solutions from mechanics. Trans. from the Greek by J. L. Heiberg and from the German by L. G. R. (Chicago, Open Court Publ. Co., 1909).

## ARCHYTAS OF TARENTUM
### (Fl. 400 B.C.)

TAYLOR (THOMAS) Political fragments of Archytas, Charondas, Zaleucus, and other ancient Pythagoreans; and, Ethical fragments of Hierocles. London, 1822.

## ARETAEUS OF CAPPADOCIA
### (Fl. A.D. 70)

*ADAMS (F.) Extant works; Greek text and translation. Sydenham Society. London, 1856.

MOFFAT (JOHN) Eight books on the causes, symptoms, and cure of acute and chronic diseases. London, 1785.

REYNOLDS (T. F.) Of the causes and signs of acute and chronic diseases. London, 1837.

## ARGENTARIUS
### (Date uncertain.)

Poetic fragments. *See* Greek Anthology (Appendix).

## ARION
### (Fl. c. 700 B.C.)

Poetic fragments. *See* "Lyra Graeca" (Appendix).

[ 71 ]

# ARISTAENETUS
(d. A.D. 358)

BROWN (THOMAS) Epistles. 9th edition. London, 1760. Reprinted in volume 1 of collected works, 1760, etc.

*KELLY (W. K.) Love epistles: literally trans. into prose. *Bohn's Class. Lib.* Bell, 1848.

> According to Smith's "Classical Dictionary", this work is wrongly ascribed to Aristaenetus. This edition also contains the poetical version noted below, and the works of Petronius, Johannes Secundus and Propertius.

SHERIDAN (R. BRINSLEY) and L. B. HALKED. Love epistles. Trans. into verse. London, 1771. Repr. *Bohn's Class. Lib.* Bell, 1848.

> "A much esteemed version."—*Lowndes's Bibliographer's Manual.*


# ARISTARCHUS
(Fl. 280-264 B.C.)

HEATH (SIR THOMAS L.) Treatise of the size and distance of the sun and moon; Greek text with translation. O.U.P., 1913.


# ARISTEAS
(His date is quite uncertain.)

LEWIS (E. D.) History of the seventy-two interpreters: to which is added, The History of the angels, and their gallantry with the daughters of men, written by Enoch, the Patriarch, London, 1715.

# ARISTIDES, SAINT

(2nd century A.D.)

HARRIS (J. R.) Apology on behalf of the Christians. C.U.P., 1891. (N.Y., Macmillan.) Vol. I of J. A. Robinson's "Text and Studies". A full translation is not given, but the notes and fragmentary translations from the Armenian, Syriac and Greek are of great value and interest.

*KAY (D. M.) Apology. *Ante-Nicene Library*. T. and T. Clark, 1897. (N.Y., Scribner.)

WALFORD (W. S.) Apology. Scott Publ. Co., 1909.

*See also* Apostolic Fathers (Appendix).

# ARISTOPHANES

(450–385 B.C.)

*Two or more comedies:*

EVERYMAN'S LIBRARY. The plays of Aristophanes. 2 vols. Dent, 1909. (N.Y., Dutton.)

> This edition contains the Acharnians; The Knights; The Birds; and, The Frogs, by J. H. Frere; The Trial of Euripides; and, The Thesmophorians, by William J. Hickie; The Clouds, by T. Mitchell; and, The Wasps, by G. Cumberland.

*FRERE (J. HOOKHAM) Plays of Aristophanes: a verse translation. (1840.) Repr. in the *Everyman's Library* (Dent), in *Bohn's Class. Lib.* (Bell), and in the

*World's Classics* (O.U.P.), 1912. (N.Y., Dutton, Macmillan and the Oxford Press.)

"The free version of Hookham Frere is almost as good as any translation in verse of an untranslatable ancient can be."—*Frederic Harrison, The Choice of Books.*

"His translation of Aristophanes cannot fail to be the most lasting memorial of his genius, and the manner in which he has successfully caught the spirit of the original comedies places him in an almost unique place as a translator."—*D.N.B.*

Further comment seems superfluous, yet it should certainly be pointed out that Frere's Aristophanes is not magnificently indecent—and the original is. Enjoyable as his version is, therefore, one is still far from knowing the true Aristophanes when one has read Frere.

PERRIN (B.) The Clouds; and Plutus: a prose translation. (N.Y., Appleton, 1904.)

**ROGERS (B. BICKLEY) Plays: a verse translation. Bell. Repr. also in the *Loeb Class.Lib.* 3 vols. Heinemann. (N.Y., Putnam.)

This great translation is issued in cheap form by Bell, in single volumes. The work is almost universally praised in superlative terms. R. G. Moulton, in his "Ancient Classical Drama", affirmed it to be "among the greatest feats in translation ever accomplished". The obituary notice of the translator in the "Classical Review" (vol. 33) concludes: "It would hardly be possible to praise too highly his achievement as a translator. At first it was the custom for reviewers of his books, as they appeared play after play, to say that he was a good second to Frere. In reality his versions are incomparably superior in every point. . . . For English readers . . . Rogers has produced the one and only version of Aristophanes."

*Single Plays:*

SHEPPARD (J. T.) The Birds; freely adapted and arranged. Cambridge, Bowes and Bowes, 1924.

> Merits special attention on account of its success as "a modern stage version".

MURRAY (GILBERT) The Frogs. Allen and Unwin, 1908. (N.Y., Oxford Press.)

> "Every lover of scholarship and good literature will hail with delight Professor Murray's new verse translation from the *Frogs* of Aristophanes."—*The Times*, Oct. 22, 1908.

> SUMMARY.—It is unfortunate that so fine a translation as Rogers's should suffer from bowdlerization, particularly in the *Lysistrata*. The most free translation of this play is that by Jack Lindsay, published by the Fanfrolico Press. This is almost unobtainable, however, so that the best advice to give Greekless readers who wish to read Aristophanes as everybody should be allowed to read him is that given by Mr. Clive Bell: learn French and then purchase or borrow a literal version in that language.

# ARISTOTLE

## (384–322 B.C.)

*Loeb Classical Library.* The Works of Aristotle. Heinemann, 1926. (N.Y., Putnam.) *In progress.*

> Contents:—*Economics,* and, *Organon,* by St. George Stock; *Nicomachean Ethics,* by H. Rackham; *Poetics,* by W. H. Fyfe; *Politics,* and, *The Athenian Constitution,* by E. Capps; *Art of Rhetoric,* by J. H. Freese.

**SMITH (J. A.) and W. D. Ross, Editors. The Complete works of Aristotle. O.U.P. *In Progress.*

> This monumental translation will eventually supersede all others. The volumes issued to date already contain such great classics as Bywater's *Poetics* and Jowett's *Politics*.

## The Nicomachean Ethics
*PETERS (F. H.) The Nicomachean ethics. (1881.) Repr. K. Paul, 1923. (N.Y., Scribner.)

> "Seems to have won recognition as the best. It is marked by terseness and felicity."—*H. Rackham.*

WELLDON (J. E. C.) Nicomachean ethics; and, Rhetoric. Macmillan, 1886.

> A literal translation praised by many scholars, some of whom, however, think it spoilt by a certain stiffness in the English.

## The Poetics
BUTCHER (S. H.) Aristotle's theory of poetry and fine art, with a translation of his Poetics. Macmillan, 1894–1902.

**BYWATER (I). The Poetics. O.U.P., 1909.

> Likely to remain for many years by far the finest translation of this work. It is included in the Oxford Translation noticed above.

## The Politics
**JOWETT (BENJAMIN) Politics. O.U.P., 1905.

> "A classic, and justly recognized as a masterpiece of English."—*Sir J. Sandys, History of Classical Scholarship, Vol.* 3, *p.* 419. Included in the Oxford Translation noticed above.

WELLDON (J. E. C.) Politics. Macmillan.

Held in considerable repute by many authorities.

### Rhetoric

**JEBB (Sir. R. C.) Rhetoric. C.U.P., 1909. (N. Y., Macmillan.)

"Open Jebb's rendering where you will, you feel that you are reading genuine English—terse, idiomatic, easy, vigorous."—*Class. Rev., Vol.* 23, *p.* 263.

WELLDON (J. E. C.) Rhetoric (bound with the Nicomachean ethics). Macmillan, 1886.

A reliable and sound version which still retains the high position it was granted on its first appearance.

### Miscellaneous Works

CRESSWELL (R.) History of animals. *Bohn's Class. Lib.* Bell, 1862.

KENYON (SIR F. G.) On the Athenian constitution; trans. with notes. Bell, 1891. (N.Y., Macmillan.)

WALLACE (Edwin) Psychology: Greek text and English translation, with intro. and notes. C.U.P., 1882. (N.Y., Macmillan.)

# ARISTOXENUS OF TARENTUM

### (Fl. 318 B.C.)

MACRAN (H. S.) Harmonics: the Greek text with translation. O.U.P., 1902.

# ARRIAN

(b. A.D. 90)

*CHINNOCK (E. J.) The Anabasis of Alexander: a literal translation. Hodder and Stoughton, 1884. Reprinted with the "Indica", and a commentary, in *Bohn's Classical Library*, 1893.

DANCEY (W.) On Coursing: the Cynegeticus of the younger Xenophon (i.e. Arrian). London, 1831.

FALCONER (W.) Voyage round the Euxine Sea. Oxford, 1805.

*McCRINDLE (J. W.) The Invasion of India by Alexander the Great, as described by Arrian, Quintus Curtius, Diodorus, Plutarch and Justin. Bell, 1893.

—— The Commerce and navigation of the Erythraean Sea; a trans. of the Periplus Maris Erythraei (ascribed to Arrian) and of Arrian's account of the voyage of Nearkhos, with notes. Thacker (Calcutta), 1879, and Bell.

ROOKE (JOHN) The History of Alexander's expedition. 2 vols. London, 1729.

> A contemporary critic says that this translation "appears to be a very just and faithful one, and to have truly represented the sense of the author".

VINCENT (WILLIAM) The Voyage of Nearchus from the Indies to the Euphrates. London, 1797, and Oxford, 1809.

*See also* Epictetus.

[ 78 ]

# ARTEMIDORUS

## (A.D. 138–180)

WOOD (ROBERT) Interpretation of dreams. London, 1644. (Fourth Edition).


# ASCLEPIADES

## (Fl. 4th cent. B.C.)

STORER (EDWARD) Windflowers of Asclepiades. Egoist Press, 1920.

> *See also* Poetic fragments in Greek Anthology (Appendix)


# ASCLEPIODOTUS

## (Fl. 1st cent. B.C.)

ILLINOIS GREEK CLUB. Tactics. *Loeb Class. Lib.* Heinemann, 1923. (N.Y., Putnam.)

> Included in the volume which contains the works of Aeneas Tacticus.


# ATHANASIUS, SAINT

## (A.D. 296–373)

BINDLEY (T. H.) On the Incarnation. R.T.S., 1903.

McLAUGHLIN (J.B.), St. Anthony the Hermit. (N.Y., Benhiser.)

NEWMAN (J. H.) Select tracts of St. Athanasius in controversy with the Arians. 2 vols. Longmans, 1895. (N.Y., Longmans.)

ROBERTSON (ARCHIBALD) On the Incarnation. D. Nutt, 1885. Also included in the select library of the *Nicene and Post-Nicene Fathers Series*. Clark. (N.Y., Scribner.)

TREATISES, historical tracts and festal epistles. 4 vols. *A Library of the Fathers Series*. J. H. and J. Parker. Oxford, 1842–1854. (N.Y., Christian Literature Society.)

*See also* Apostolic Fathers (Appendix).

## ATHENAEUS

(Fl. A.D. 230)

GULICK (C. B.)The Deipnosophists; or, The Banquet of the learned. 6 vols. *Loeb Class. Lib.* Heinemann, 1927. (N.Y., Putnam.) *In progress.*

YONGE (C. D.) The Deipnosophists; or, The Banquet of the learned: literally translated, with an appendix of poetical fragments rendered into English verse. *Bohn's Class. Lib.* Bell, 1854. (N.Y., Macmillan.)

## ATHENAGORAS

(Fl. 2nd cent. A.D.)

*See* Apostolic Fathers (Appendix).

# AURELIUS

(Marcus Aurelius Antoninus, A.D. 121–180)

CASAUBON (MERIC) The Golden book of Marcus
Aurelius. (1634). Repr. in the *Everyman's Library*.
Dent, 1906. (N.Y., Dutton.)

"This, the first English translation, albeit involved and
periphrastic, is not without dignity or scholarship, though
James Thomson in 1747 says that 'it is everywhere rude,
and unpolished, and often mistakes the author's meaning';
while the Foulis Press translators of 1742 find fault with
its 'intricate and antiquated style'. "—*C. R. Haines, in his
preface to the Loeb Lib. translation.*

COLLIER (JEREMY) Meditations. 1701. Repr. rev. by
Alice Zimmern in *The Camelot Series*. Scott, 1887.

The too colloquial and familiar style of this well-known
translation has occasioned some crushing criticisms, viz.:
"A very coarse copy of an excellent original"—J. Thomson,
1747; "It abounds with so many vulgarities, anilities and
even ludicrous expressions that one cannot now read it
with any patience"—R. Graves, 1792; "Written in the
jaunty and obtrusively familiar style affected by the fine
gentlemen of the close of the seventeenth century"—G.
Long, 1862. Despite the unanimity of opinion displayed
by these critics, Jeremy Collier's translation has nevertheless pleased many readers, of whom Matthew Arnold
is the most important. The latter, indeed, says in his
essay on Marcus Aurelius that Collier's version "deserves
respect for its genuine spirit and vigour, the spirit and
vigour of the age of Dryden. [Collier's] warmth of feeling
gave to his style an impetuosity and rhythm which from
Long's style are absent." In the reprint noted above the
editor has revised those portions which show that Collier
was imperfectly acquainted with the Greek original.

*Haines (C. R.) The Meditations. *Loeb. Class. Lib.* Heinemann, 1920. (N.Y., Putnam.)

> "For accuracy and faithfulness in the sense of closeness to the original, there is no doubt, I think, that Mr. Haines surpasses all his competitors. None the less, I imagine that most English readers, innocent of pedantry and of Greek, would vote for Dr. Rendall's version as the more attractive and the more impressive."—*R. G. Bury, Class. Rev., Vol.* 32, *p.* 33.

Jackson (John) Meditations. *World's Classics.* O.U.P., 1906.

*Long (George) Meditations. 1862. Repr. in *Bell's Popular Library*, 1900, and Harrap, 1926. (N.Y., Burt; Harcourt.)

> This is undoubtedly the most widely read translation and has, indeed, been called "The authorized version".

*Moor (James) and Thomas Hutcheson. The Meditations: a new rendering based on the Foulis translation by Moor and Hutcheson, of 1742, by G. W. Chrystal. Schulze. Edinburgh, 1902.

> Dr. Rendall thinks this the choicest alike in form and content of all translations of "The Meditations".

**Rendall (G. H.) The Meditations. (1898.) Repr. in the *Golden Treasury Series*. Macmillan, 1901.

> "The translator is in thorough sympathy with his subject; he is well equipped, as is shown in the introduction, with the learning which is required for understanding him, and he is, moreover, a master of an English style which in its grave and quiet beauty reflects the tone of thought of Aurelius far better than his own perplexed and crabbed Greek."—*J. B. Mayor, Class. Rev., Vol.* 12, *p.* 315.

# BABRIUS
### (Fl. 1st cent. A.D.)

DAVIES (JAMES) Fables: trans. into English verse. Lockwood, 1860.

*See also* Aesop.


# BACCHYLIDES
### (Fl. 470 B.C.)

*JEBB (Sir R. C.) Poems and fragments; with intro., notes and a prose trans. C.U.P., 1905. (N.Y., Macmillan.)
> "The translation is faithful, and renders excellently the spirit of the original."—*Class. Rev., Vol.* 20, *p.* 170.

POSTE (E). Poems: a prose translation. Macmillan, 1898.

WAY (A. S.) The Odes: a verse translation. Macmillan, 1929.

*See also* "Lyra Graeca", and Howe and Harrer (Appendix).


# BARNABAS
### (Fl. A.D. 38)

*See* Apostolic Fathers (Appendix).


# BASIL, SAINT
### (A.D. 329–379)

CLARKE (W. L. K.) Ascetic works. *Trans. of Christian Lit. Series.* S.P.C.K., 1925. (N.Y., Macmillan.)

DEFERRARI (ROY J.) Letters. 4 vols. *Loeb Class. Lib.*
Heinemann, 1926. (N.Y., Putnam.) *In progress.*

JACKSON (B.) The Homilies and the Letters. *Nicene and
Post-Nicene Fathers, Second series, vol.* 8. Clark,
1895. (N.Y., Scribner.)

> See Apostolic Fathers (Appendix).

# BATRACHOMYOMACHIA

BARLOW (J.) The Battle of the frogs and the mice: trans.
into English verse. Methuen, 1894.

*CHAPMAN (GEORGE) Batrachomyomachia; or, the
Battle of the frogs and the mice: a mock epic.
(1625.) Repr. by J. R. Smith. London, 1858, and
Chatto and Windus, 1904.

*EVELYN-WHITE (H. G.) Batrachomyomachia. *Loeb
Class. Lib.* Heinemann, 1915. (N.Y., Putnam.)

> This is included in the volume which also contains a
> prose translation of Hesiod's works and the Homeric
> Hymns.

PARNELL (THOMAS). The Battle of the frogs and the
mice: trans. into Eng. heroic verse. (1717.) Repr.
with Pope's Homer. *Bohn's Class. Lib.* Bell, 1902.

# BION

(Fl. 280 B.C.)
See Theocritus, Bion and Moschus.

# CALLIMACHUS

## (d. 240 B.C.)

BANKS (J.) Poems and fragments. Literally trans. with a metrical version by Tytler. *Bohn's Class. Lib.* Bell, 1848.

> Included in the volume which contains the works of Hesiod and Theognis.

DODD (WILLIAM) Poems. London, 1755.

*MAIR (A. W.) Hymns and fragments. *Loeb Class. Lib.* Heinemann, 1921. (N.Y., Putnam.)

> Included in the volume which contains the works of Lycophron and Aratus.

*TYTLER (H. W.) Poems and fragments. London, 1793. Repr. in *Bohn's Class. Lib.* Bell, 1848.

> Dr. Tytler, with a view to preparing himself for translation, compared every line of the "Iliad" with Pope's version.
>
> "William Dodd's translation has considerable merit, but H. W. Tytler's is better."—*J. Banks.*
> See also Greek Anthology, and Howe and Harrer (Appendix).

# CALLINUS

## (Fl. 700 B.C.)

See Howe and Harrer (Appendix).

# CALLISTRATUS

## (Fl. 3rd cent. B.C.)

See Howe and Harrer (Appendix).

# CEBES

## (2nd cent. A.D.)

*CLARK (R. T.) The Table; or, The Picture of human life. *New Univ. Lib.* Routledge, 1909. (N.Y., Dutton.)

> Included in the volume which contains the works of Theophrastus and Herodas.

**DAVIES (JOHN) The Emblem of human life (The Table). London, 1670. Repr. Glasgow, Thomson, 1901.

> The lithographic reprint gives the student an opportunity of becoming acquainted with a very interesting seventeenth-century translation of this famous allegory.

HEALEY (J.) The Table. London, 1610.

GUTHRIE (KENNETH SYLVAN) The Greek Pilgrim's Progress (The Table). (N.Y., Platonist Press.)

SCOTT (THOMAS) The Table: a translation into verse. London, 1754.

> This dull version is of little value.

WARREN (R.) The Table. Cambridge, 1699.


# CHARITON

## (c. 4th cent. A.D.)

ANONYMOUS. The Loves of Chaereas and Callirrhoe. 2 vols. London, 1764.

> This anonymous translation was made from an Italian version.

# CHARIXENA
### (Date uncertain)

Poetic fragments. *See* "Lyra Graeca" (Appendix).


# CHARONDAS
### (6th cent. B.C.)

TAYLOR (THOMAS) Poetical fragments of Archytas, Charondas, Zaleucus and other ancient Pythagoreans, and ethical fragments of Hierocles. London, 1822.


# CHRYSOSTOM, SAINT JOHN
### (A.D. 347–407)

COTTON (W. C.), "Members of the English Church", and others. Homilies. 15 vols. *Library of the Fathers*. J. H. and J. PARKER. Oxford, 1839 to 1852.

> *See also* Apostolic Fathers (Appendix).


# CLEANTHES THE STOIC
### (3rd cent. B.C.)

BLAKENEY (E. H.) Hymn: Greek text, with notes and trans. Sheldon Press, 1920.

*CROSSLEY (H.) The Hymn of Cleanthes. *Golden Treasury Series*. Macmillan, 1903.

> This translation is included in the volume which contains the works of Epictetus.
> *See also* Howe and Harrer (Appendix).

# CLEMENT OF ALEXANDRIA

### (d. A.D. 220)

BUTTERWORTH (G. W.) The Exhortation to the Greeks, The Rich man's salvation, and a short fragment entitled "To the newly baptised". *Loeb Class. Lib.* Heinemann. (N.Y., Putnam.)

> *See also* Apostolic Fathers (Appendix).

# COLUTHUS

### (6th cent. A.D.)

BELOE (WILL) The Rape of Helene. London, 1786.

★MAIR (A. W.) The Rape of Helen: a prose translation. *Loeb Class. Lib.* Heinemann, 1928. (N.Y., Putnam.)

> Included in a volume also containing translations of Oppian and Tryphiodorus.

★MEEN (H.) The Rape of Helen. 1780. Repr. in Vol. 20 of Chalmers's "Works of the English Poets", 1810.

> This version, sometimes erroneously attributed to Fawkes, was published as an appendix to that writer's translation of Apollonius Rhodius.

SHERBURNE (EDWARD) The Rape of Helen: a verse translation. London, 1651.

# CORINNA

### (Fl. 490 B.C.)

Poetic fragments. *See* "Lyra Graeca" (Appendix).

# CRINAGORUS OF MYTILENE

## (Fl. A.D. 10)

Poetic fragments. *See* Greek Anthology (Appendix).


# CTESIAS OF CNIDUS

## (Fl. 400 B.C.)

McCRINDLE (J. W.) Ancient India: a translation of the abridgment of his "Indika", by Photius, and of the fragments of that work preserved in other writings. Trubner, 1882.


# CYRIL, SAINT

## (Bishop of Jerusalem A.D. 315–386)

NEWMAN (J. H.) Catechetical lectures: *A Library of the Fathers*. J. H. and J. Parker. Oxford, 1839.

*See also* Apostolic Fathers (Appendix).


# DEMETRIUS PHALEREUS

## (345–307 B.C.)

ROBERTS (W. RHYS) On style: the Greek text of "De Elocutione", with intro., trans., etc. C.U.P., 1902. (N.Y., Macmillan.)

Also in the *Loeb Classical Library* (1927), in the volume containing Aristotle's *Poetics* and Longinus' *On the sublime*.

# DEMOSTHENES

(383–322 B.C.)

**KENNEDY (C. RANN) The Orations. 5 vols. *Bohn's Class. Lib.* Bell, 1852. Repr. of "De Corona", and "Philippic and Olynthian Orations" in *Everyman's Lib.* Dent, 1911. (N.Y., Dutton, and in Pocket Series, Mackay.)

*LELAND (THOMAS) All the orations of Demosthenes pronounced to excite the Athenians against Philip, King of Macedon, and on occasions of public deliberation. Also the orations of Dinarchus against Demosthenes and the orations of Aeschines and Demosthenes on the Crown. 3 vols. London, 1763 and 1824. Repr. 2 vols., N.Y., Lamb, 1908. The oration on the Crown was also reprinted in London, in 1853, by H. G. Bohn.

> Contemporary criticism of this work was very eulogistic, e.g.: "So well executed that we do not expect to see any other writer do the same justice to the eloquence of Demosthenes"; and again, "a work of extraordinary merit; the translation is executed with a spirit and energy nearly equal to the original and the notes are very valuable".

LOEB CLASSICAL LIBRARY. Private orations, trans. by G. M. CALHOUN; and De Corona and De falsa legatione: trans. by C. A. and J. H. VINCE. Heinemann, 1926. (N.Y., Putnam.)

*PICKARD-CAMBRIDGE (A. W.) Public orations. 2 vols O.U.P., 1912.

> "This version is very good: faithful, clear, responsive, scholarly, and, in short, worthy of his name."—*Class. Rev., Vol.* 28, *p.* 142.

# DIAGORAS

### (Fl. 430 B.C.)

Poetic fragments. *See* "Lyra Graeca" (Appendix).


# DIDACHE ; OR, TEACHING OF THE TWELVE APOSTLES

*See* Apostolic Fathers (Appendix).


# DIO CASSIUS

### (b. A.D. 155)

*CARY (E.) Roman history. 9 vols. *Loeb Class. Lib.* Heinemann, 1925. (N.Y., Putnam.)

FOWLER (H. B.) Dio's Rome. 6 vols. Pafraets Book Co., Troy, N.Y., 1905.

> Cary's translation in the *Loeb* (noted above) is based on this well-known version of Fowler's; it will be rightly preferred by most students, since it embodies the latest textual emendations and is a valuable revision of Fowler's work.

MANNING. The History of Dion Cassius, abridged by Xiphilin. 2 vols. London, 1704.


# DIO CHRYSOSTOM

### (Fl. 1st cent. A.D.)

WAKEFIELD (GILBERT) Select essays. London, 1800.

# DIODORUS SICULUS

(*c.* 50 B.C.–A.D. 20)

BOOTH (G.) The Historical library, containing the antiquities of Egypt, Asia, Africa, Greece and Europe. London, 1700 and 1814.

> "Held in considerable estimation."—*Moss, Manual of Classical Bibliography.*

COGAN (Thomas) The History of the world. London, 1653.

STOCKER (THOMAS) History of the successors of Alexander, surnamed The Great. London, 1568.

# DIOGENES LAERTIUS

(Fl. 2nd cent. A.D.)

*HICKS (R. D.) The Lives of eminent philosophers. 2 vols. *Loeb Class. Lib.* Heinemann, 1925. (N.Y., Putnam.)

YONGE (C. D.) The Lives and opinions of ancient philosophers. *Bohn's Class. Lib.* Bell, 1853. (N.Y., Harcourt.)

# DION CASSIUS

*See* Dio Cassius.

# DION CHRYSOSTUM

*See* Dio Chrysostom.

# DIONYSIUS ALEXANDRINUS

## (Fl. A.D. 300)

*FELTOE (CHARLES LETT) Letters and treatises. *Trans. of Christian Lit. Series*, I. S.P.C.K., 1918. (N.Y., Macmillan.)

LOFTUS (DUDLEY) Syrus: a commentary on St. John the Evangelist. Dublin, 1672.

TWINE (THOMAS) The Surveye of the world. London, 1572.

*See also* Apostolic Fathers (Appendix).


# DIONYSIUS OF HALICARNASSUS

## (Fl. 29 B.C.)

*ROBERTS (W. RHYS) On literary composition. Macmillan, 1910. (N.Y., Macmillan.)

*—— Three literary letters. C.U.P., 1901. (N.Y., Macmillan.)

SPELMAN (EDWARD) Roman antiquities. 4 vols. London. 1758.

> The following estimate is higher than the scholarship of to-day would place Spelman's work, yet those who have access to it will find Spelman's translation both reliable and good to read. "Faithful and elegant; he has not only rendered the sense of his author with exactness, but has

caught his spirit and manner; his style is smooth and flowing, his language in general, pure and elegant; in a word, without any partiality to his translation, it deserves ... to be ranked among the best in the English language."— *A contemporary critic quoted in Moss's Manual of Bibliography.*

*See* Longinus for the treatise "On the Sublime," now generally attributed to Dionysius.

## DIONYSIUS THE AREOPAGITE

(A.D. 480–520)

ROLT (C. E.) On the divine names and mystical theology. *Trans. of Christian Lit. Series*. S.P.C.K., 1920. (N.Y., Macmillan.)

## ECHEMBROTUS

(Fl. 586 B.C.)

Poetic fragments. *See* "Lyra Graeca" (Appendix).

## EMPEDOCLES OF AGRIGENTUM

(d. 430 B.C.)

LEONARD (W. E.) Fragments: trans. into English verse. Chicago, Open Court Publishing Co., 1908.

## ENOCH THE PATRIARCH

*See* Aristeas.

# EPICTETUS

(b. *c.* A.D. 50)

CARTER (ELIZABETH) The Works of Epictetus which
are now extant: discourses in 4 books. Encheiridion, fragments. 1758. Repr., edited by W. H. D.
ROUSE, in *Everyman's Library*. Dent, 1910. (N.Y.,
Dutton.)

> "The translation of Mrs. Carter is good, and perhaps no
> Englishman of that time would have made a better trans-
> lation."—*George Long, Preface to Bohn's Popular Library.*

CROSSLEY (H.) The Golden sayings, with the Hymn
of Cleanthes. *Golden Treasury Series.* Macmillan,
1903. (N.Y., Macmillan.)

*LONG (GEORGE) The Discourses; with the Encheiri-
dion and fragments, trans. with notes. *Bohn's
Popular Library*. Bell, 1877. (N.Y., Burt.)

*MATHESON (P. E.) The Discourses and the Manual.
O.U.P., 1916.

> "An excellent translation, which marks a notable advance
> on its predecessors."—*A. C. Pearson, Class. Rev., Vol.* 31,
> *p.* 172.

> "The translation as a whole and almost all of the intro-
> duction are admirable."—*A. Y. Campbell, Year's Work
> in Class. Studies,* 1919.

> "A most pleasant and graceful version."—*W. A. Old-
> father, Preface to Loeb. Class. Lib.*

OLDFATHER (W. A.) The Discourses as reported by
Arrian, the Manual, and fragments. 2 vols. *Loeb
Class. Lib.* Heinemann, 1926. (N.Y., Putnam.)

ROLLESTON (T. W. H.) The Encheiridion. 1881. Repr. in the *Camelot Classics*, 1888, and in *Lubbock's 100 Best Books Series*, 1891. (N.Y., Simmons; New and rev. edn., Nelson.)

# EPICURUS
### (342–270 B.C.)

*BAILEY (CYRIL) Extant remains, with short, critical apparatus, translation and notes. O.U.P., 1926.

CHARLETON (WALTER) Morals; collected, partly out of his owne Greek text in Diogenes Laertius and partly out of the rhapsodies of Marcus Aurelius, Plutarch, Cicero and Seneca. (1656.) Repr. Peter Davies, 1926.

DIGBY (JOHN) Morals. London, 1712.

# ERATOSTHENES SCHOLASTICUS
### (*c.* 275–195 B.C.)

Poetic fragments. *See* Greek Anthology (Appendix).

# EUCLID
### (Fl. 300 B.C.)

HEATH (SIR T. L.) The Twelve books of Euclid's Elements, trans. from the text of Heiberg, With intro. and comm. 3 vols. C.U.P., 1908 and 1926. (N.Y., Macmillan.)

The standard translation from the standard text.

# EUMATHIUS

*See* Eustathius.


# EUNAPIUS

### (b. A.D. 347)

WRIGHT (W. CAVE) Lives of the philosophers. Trans. and bound with Philostratus, Lives of the sophists. *Loeb Class. Lib.* Heinemann, 1922. (N.Y., Putnam.)


# EUPOLIS

### (b. 446 B.C.)

WESLEY (C.) Hymn to the Creator. 1813. *In British Poets*, Vol. 88, 1822.


# EURIPIDES

### (480–406 B.C.)

*COLERIDGE (E. P.) Ten plays: a literal translation in prose. *Bell's Class. Trans.* 1891. (N.Y., Harcourt.)

*MURRAY (GILBERT) Plays. 2 vols. Allen and Unwin, 1911. (N.Y., published separately by the Oxford Press and by Longmans.)

A new one-volume edition of the *Oresteia* was published by Allen and Unwin in 1928.

"Mr. Gilbert Murray's renderings of several plays of Euripides into rhymed English verse seem sometimes to impart a modern element into interpretation of the poet, but they are none the less welcome as helping to promote the appreciation of Euripides by the modern mind."— *Sir J. E. Sandys in The Year's Work in Class. Studies,* 1907.

"Professor Gilbert Murray has translated the *Rhesus* into English rhyming verse; the translation has all the charm which is always associated with his work, and when (as happens rather often) he appears to read a good deal into the Greek, he almost gives his reader something more than the original."—*A. W. Pickard-Cambridge in The Year's Work in Class. Studies,* 1913.

Professor Murray's translations have been the subject of the most superlative praise and the most violent abuse. They annoy some scholars who are intolerant of the slightest alteration of the text; they please some who find in them a dramatic quality which fits as well with the original as can be expected; yet again some find the versification spineless, and others see in it a perfect adaptation of the smooth, monotonous beauty of Swinburne's melodies. It follows, therefore, that being so important as to provoke such strenuous discussion they must be read by all who wish to read Euripides in English; yet, in justice to the scholarly objections hurled at them by critics too authoritative to be disregarded, the serious student should also read an excellent prose version such as E. P. Coleridge's noted above, or A. S. Way's verse translation in the *Loeb Library.*

POTTER (R.) The Tragedies of Euripides. 2 vols. 1781–83. Repr. in *Morley's Universal Library.* Routledge, 1887. (N.Y., Dutton.)

> Highly praised in its time, this blank verse translation, of which a selection is reprinted in the *Everyman's Library,* reads rather pompously to those accustomed to Murray's or Way's melodious lines. Nevertheless the version has dignity and dramatic excitement.

**WAY (A. S.) Plays: a verse translation. (1894–8.) Repr., rev. edn., in *Loeb Class. Lib.* 4 vols. Heinemann, 1912–1923. (N.Y., Putnam.)

> "The admirable work of Mr. A. S. Way has removed what was at once a reproach to scholarship and a difficulty in practical teaching—the absence of an adequate translation of Euripides. . . . Mr. Way follows all the technicalities of verse fluctuation, without the force or flow of the English poem being allowed to flag."—*R. G. Moulton in Ancient Classical Drama.*

## Alcestis

BROWNING (ROBERT) Balaustion's adventure, including a transcript from Euripides' Alcestis. (1871.) Repr. in all editions of Browning's complete poetical works, Smith Elder, O.U.P., etc. (N.Y., Crowell, 1875, etc.)

## The Bacchanals

LUCAS (D. W.) The Bacchae: the Greek text, together with a prose translation. Cambridge, Bowes and Bowes, 1930.

> The text was edited for a special series of performances at Cambridge, and the translation was deemed to be eminently suitable for the modern stage.

*MILMAN (DEAN) The Bacchanals: a verse translation. (1865). Repr. with Shelley's version of the Cyclops, in the *Everyman's* edition. Dent. (N.Y., Dutton.)

## The Cyclops

SHELLEY (PERCY B.) The Cyclops: a verse translation, (1819). Repr. in all editions of Shelley's works, and also, with Milman's version of the Bacchanals in the *Everyman's* edition. Dent. (N.Y., Dutton.)

> The departures from the original are fully compensated by the rare quality of the translator's verse. The following estimates are typical: "Admirably lithe and graceful English verse. No rendering from Greek literature can possibly be more animated or more strong in its lightness."—*Prof. Edw. Dowden, in Life of Shelley.* "While revising the version of the *Cyclops*, I have felt again, and more keenly, the old delight of wonder at its matchless grace of unapproachable beauty, its strength, ease, delicate simplicity and sufficiency: the birthmark and native quality of all Shelley's translation."—*A. C. Swinburne, in Notes on the Texts of Shelley.*

SHEPPARD (J. T.) The Cyclops: freely arranged and adapted. C.U.P., 1923. (N.Y., Macmillan.)

> Merits special attention on account of its success as a "modern stage version".

## *Hecuba*

SHEPPARD (J. T.) Hecuba. O.U.P., 1927.

> A metrical version of great merit, retaining, like this translator's version of the *Frogs* of Aristophanes, the dramatic quality of the play.

# EUSEBIUS
### (A.D. 264–340)

*McGIFFERT (A. C.) and E. C. RICHARDSON. Works. *Nicene and Post-Nicene Fathers: second series.* Clark, 1890. (N.Y., Scribner.)

## *The Ecclesiastical History*

*LAKE (KIRSOPP) Ecclesiastical history. 2 vols. *Loeb Class. Lib.* Heinemann, 1926. (N.Y., Putnam.)

LAWLOR (H. J.) and J. E. L. OULTON. Ecclesiastical history, and, The Martyrs of Palestine. S.P.C.K., 1927. (N.Y., Macmillan.)

### Miscellaneous Works

CONYBEARE (F. C.) On the life of Apollonius of Tyana by Philostratus. *Loeb. Class. Lib.* Heinemann, 1926. (N.Y., Putnam.)

> Included in the volume containing a translation of the life of Apollonius.

FERRAR (W. J.) Proof of the Gospel. 2 vols. S.P.C.K., 1920. (N.Y., Macmillan.)

GIFFORD (E. H.) Preparation for the Gospel. O.U.P., 1903.

> *See also* Apostolic Fathers (Appendix).


# EUSTATHIUS
### (Fl. 12th cent. A.D.)

ANONYMOUS. Ismene and Ismenias. Trans. from the French version of L. H. Le Moine. London, 1788.


# EVAGRIUS
### (b. A.D. 536)

ANONYMOUS. History of the Church, A.D. 431–594. *Bohn's Eccles. Lib.* Bell, 1854.


# FATHERS, THE
*See* Apostolic Fathers (Appendix).

# GALEN

(A.D. 130–200)

BROCK (A. J.) On the natural faculties. *Loeb Class. Lib.* Heinemann, 1916. (N.Y., Putnam.)

> This translation is "spirited, idiomatic, scholarly, and often happy; thus it is very readable by itself."—*Class. Rev.*, Vol. 31, *p.* 101.

# GREGORY NAZIANZEN, SAINT

(Fl. A.D. 380)

BROWNING (E. BARRETT) Soul and body: a poem.

> This translation will be found in an article entitled "Greek Christian Poets", which was contributed by Mrs. Browning to the "Athenæum", 1842. It is reprinted in the Oxford University Press edition of Mrs. Browning's poems.

KING (C. W.) Two invectives against Julian the Emperor. *Bohn's Class. Lib.* Bell, 1888.

> *See also* Apostolic Fathers (Appendix).

# GREGORY THAUMATURGUS

(213?–270?)

METCALFE (W.) Address to Origen. *Translations of Christian Literature Series.* S.P.C.K., 1920. (N.Y., Macmillan.)

> First issued in 1907 as "Origen the Teacher."
>
> *See also* Apostolic Fathers (Appendix).

# HELIODORUS
(Fl. end of 4th cent. A.D.)

SMITH (ROWLAND) The Ethiopics; or, The Adventures of Theagenes and Chariclea. *Bohn's Class. Lib.* Bell, 1882. (N.Y., Macmillan.)

> Included in the volume which also contains the Greek romances of Longus and Achilles Tatius.

**UNDERDOWNE (THOMAS) The Ethiopian history. (1587). Repr. with an intro. by G. Saintsbury in *The Abbey Classics*. Chapman and Dodd, 1922. (Boston, Small); also, Rev. and partly re-written by F. A. WRIGHT. *Broadway Translations*. Routledge. (N.Y., Dutton.)

> "An important example of Elizabethan prose, remarkable for rhythm and poetic vigour; but Underdowne's Greek scholarship was slight."—*D.N.B.*
>
> ". . . Underdowne fails as a translator, because his ignorance of Greek and Latin was frank and magnificent. . . . (He) was a poor translator but a great writer. . . . His version, then, is purely English, untouched of Greek or foreign influence. Gifted with an unerring taste of narrative, endowed with a rare sense of the cadences of prose, Underdowne was more than most of his contemporaries, a maker of English prose."—*Charles Whibley, Preface to a reprint in The Tudor Translations Series.*
>
> "Underdowne's translation, although I cannot be quite so enthusiastic about it as my friend Mr. Charles Whibley is, has considerable attractions."—*Professor G. Saintsbury, Preface to reprint in The Abbey Classics Series.*

# HERACLITUS OF EPHESUS
(Fl. 513 B.C.)

PATRICK (G. T. W.) Fragments of the work on nature; trans. from the Greek text of Bywater. Baltimore, Murray, 1889.

# HERMES TRISMEGISTUS

(*c.* 1st cent. A.D.)

EVERARD (DR.) The Divine Pymander of Hermes. London, 1894.

SCOTT (WALTER) The Ancient Greek and Latin writings which contain religious or philosophic teachings ascribed to Hermes Trismegistus. Edited with English translations and notes. O.U.P., 1925.

*See also* Apostolic Fathers (Appendix).

# HERODAS

*See* Herondas.

# HERODIAN

(Fl. A.D. 200)

HART (J.) Herodian's history of his own times. London, 1749 and 1789.

SMYTH (NICHOLAS) History of the Roman Empire, A.D. 180–238. London, 1629.

# HERODOTUS

(*c.* 484–425 B.C.)

CARY (HENRY) The History: a literal version. *Bohn's Class. Lib.* Bell, 1843. (N.Y., Macmillan.)

**\*\*GODLEY** (A. D.) The History. 4 vols. *Loeb Class. Lib.* Heinemann, 1920–1924. (N.Y., Putnam.)

> "A translation of Herodotus as nearly perfect as a translation can be . . . and not likely to be superseded."—
> *R. W. Livingstone in Class. Rev., Vol.* 36.
> "The best existing version of Herodotus. . . . Mr. Godley's exquisite version."—*J. C. Squire in Books Reviewed, pp.* 159–165.

**MACAULAY** (G. C.) The Works of Herodotus. 2 vols. Macmillan, 1890. (N.Y., Macmillan.)

**\*RAWLINSON** (G.) The History. (1858.) Repr. in the *Everyman's Library.* 2 vols. Dent, 1910. (N.Y., Dutton.) Repr., N.Y., Scribner, 1895.

> This is undoubtedly the standard version, and has been highly praised by eminent scholars. "Rawlinson's Herodotus, like Jowett's Plato, Jebb's Sophocles and Butcher and Lang's Odyssey, is become well-nigh an English classic."—*E. H. Blakeney in preface to reprint in the Everyman's Library.*

**?RICH (BARNABY)?** The Famous history of Herodotus. (1584.) Repr. in *Tudor Translations,* 2nd Series. Edited by Leonard Whibley. Constable, 1924. (N.Y., Knopf.)

> A part of this work entitled "Euterpe" was reprinted in 1888, with a preface by Andrew Lang, published by David Nutt. "He faces the Latin with a confidence that is sometimes indifferent to the literal meaning, but his native wit pulls him through. . . . The language is colloquial, slang is frequent, proverbs abound. . . . We may say that his narrative is all the better for the free rendering which he gives. . . . With all his freedom he is not inconsistent with his original."—*Leonard Whibley, in preface to the reprint in the Tudor Translations Series.*

# HERONDAS

(Fl. 3rd cent. B.C.)

*BUCK (MITCHELL S.) The Mimes: completely rendered into English. N.Y., Brown, Nicholas L., 1921.

CLARK (R. T.) Mimes; with Theophrastus' Characters and The Tablet of Cebes. *New Univ. Lib.* Routledge, 1909. (N.Y., Dutton.)

**HEADLAM (WALTER) Mimes, trans. with notes, commentary, etc. O.U.P., 1923. (N.Y., Oxford Press, and Macmillan.)

SHARPLEY (H.) A Realist of the Aegean; a verse translation of the Mimes. Nutt, 1906.

*SYMONDS (J. A.) A Prose translation of the six poems of Herondas which have come down to us. Repr. in "Studies of the Greek Poets". A. and C. Black, 1893.

# HESIOD

(Fl. 735 B.C.)

BANKS (J.) The Works of Hesiod: a literal translation, with a metrical version by Elton. *Bohn's Class. Lib.* Bell, 1897.

> This work is bound with the works of Callimachus and Theognis.

CHAPMAN (GEORGE) The Works and days, and The Georgics. (1618.) Repr. by J. R. Smith, 1858, and

Chatto and Windus, 1920, and in all complete editions of Chapman's Poetical works.

"This, like all Chapman's work, is poetical and spirited, but often very obscure to modern readers, though it constantly cites the original in footnotes."—*Mahaffy's History of Greek Literature.*

*ELTON (C. A.) The Complete works of Hesiod: a verse translation. (1812.) Repr. in *Bohn's Class. Lib.* Bell, 1848.

"The best . . . translation of Hesiod is that of Elton, who knew his predecessors well and gives us scholarly renderings of the 'Works' in heroic rhymes and of the other two poems in blank verse."—*Mahaffy's History of Greek Literature.*

EVELYN-WHITE (H. G.) Works: a prose version. *Loeb Class. Lib.* Heinemann, 1920. (N.Y., Putnam.)

Bound with the volume which also contains the Homeric Hymns.

*MAIR (A. W.) The Poems and fragments done into prose, with notes, etc. *Oxford Translations Series.* O.U.P., 1910.

## HIEROCLES

(Fl. 5th cent. A.D.)

**BUBB (CHARLES CLINCH) The Jests of Hierocles and Philagrius. *Privately printed.* Cleveland, Ohio, Rowfant Club Co., 1920.

*HALL (JOHN) Upon the golden verses of the Pythagoreans. London, 1657.

JOHNSON (SAMUEL) The Jests of Hierocles. Contributed to "The Gentleman's Magazine", 1741.

RAYNER (WILLIAM) Commentary on the golden verses of the Pythagoreans. Norwich, 1797.

ROWE (NICHOLAS) Commentary on the golden verses of the Pythagoreans. Glasgow, 1756. Repr. Theosophical Publ. Co., London, 1906.

> This version was made from the French of Dacier.

*STANLEY (THOMAS) Commentary on the golden verses of the Pythagoreans. London, 1701.

> This translation is contained in Stanley's "History of Philosophy".

TAYLOR (THOMAS) Ethical fragments. London, 1822.

> Contained in the volume entitled "Political fragments of Archytas, Charondas, Zaleucus, and other ancient Pythagoreans."

# HIPPOCRATES
## (460–357 B.C.)

ADAMS (FRANCIS) The Genuine works of Hippocrates. 2 vols. (1886.) Repr. N.Y., 1891.

> "Adams's well-known translation is the work of a man of sense. The translation is literal and generally good, but is occasionally misleading."—*W. H. S. Jones, in the preface to his translation in the Loeb. Class. Lib.*

*JONES (W. H. S.) Ancient medicine. 3 vols. *Loeb Class. Lib.* Heinemann, 1923–1927. (N.Y., Putnam.)

# HIPPOLYTUS

(d. A.D. 230)

*See* Apostolic Fathers (Appendix).

# HOMER

(Between 1050 and 850 B.C.)

*The Iliad and the Odyssey together.*

BRYANT (WILLIAM CULLEN) The Iliad and the Odyssey: a blank verse translation. Boston, Houghton, 1870. Repr. frequently.

> On the whole a far more successful version than Cowper's, which was in the same metre. "While giving his readers the genuine spirit of Homer, Bryant has also given them one of the finest specimens of pure Saxon English in our literature."—*John Bigelow, in the American Men of Letters Series.*

BUTLER (SAMUEL) The Iliad and the Odyssey: a prose translation. (1898.) 2 vols. Repr. Cape, 1920. (N.Y., Dutton; Longmans.)

> "It is usual to talk about Butler's Homeric translations as if his *Iliad* and his *Odyssey* were of a piece. Actually the two are . . . distinct in tone. . . . Through the *Iliad* he manages to keep serious and to produce what is probably the best English prose translation of it existing, but in the *Odyssey* he becomes again the urchin of literature. . . . In prose, Butler's *Iliad*, though not ideal, has yet to be surpassed. . . . In the *Odyssey*, Butler's diction is always bald, often coarse, sometimes vulgar."—*F. L. Lucas in Authors Dead and Living.*
>
> "Butler's *Odyssey* is, in fact, a very fine prose translation, though it is not quite so fine as his *Iliad*, because it was more wilful. . . . Butler has enriched us with a Homer that is a simple, vivid, and fascinating tale. . . . Soon it will find its way into the nursery."—*J. Middleton Murry in Pencillings.*

**\*\*CHAPMAN (GEORGE) The Iliad and the Odyssey. (1612.) Repr. in the *Temple Classics*. 4 vols. Dent 1898; in 2 vols. Chatto and Windus; etc. (N.Y., Scribner; Dutton, etc.)**

"Chapman, poet as he is, is rather archaic for ordinary readers and too loose for scholarly readers."—*Frederic Harrison in The Choice of Books*.

"He [Chapman] would have made a great epic poet, if indeed he has not abundantly shown himself to be one; for his Homer is not so properly a translation as the stories of Achilles and Ulysses re-written."—*Charles Lamb in Specimens of English Dramatic Poets*.

Professor Saintsbury still thinks "Chapman the best version we have. His version," he says, "with all its faults, outlived the popularity of Pope's . . . and is likely to survive all the attempts made with us. I speak with all humility, but as having learnt Homer from Homer himself. . . . Either I have no skill in criticism, and have been reading Greek for fifty years to none effect, or Chapman is far nearer Homer than any modern translation in any modern language."—*Saintsbury's Elizabethan Literature*.

"His knowledge of Greek was not impeccable. Errors due to ignorance or haste are not infrequent. . . . If Chapman, the scholar, sometimes nodded, Chapman, the poet, was ever awake, and his version of Homer will ever remain one among the masterpieces of his age and country."—*Charles Whibley in Camb. Hist. Eng. Lit., Vol. 4, p. 22*.

**COWPER (WILLIAM) The Iliad and the Odyssey: a blank verse translation. (1791.) The Odyssey repr. in the *Everyman's Library*. Dent, 1916. (N.Y., Dutton.) The Iliad and the Odyssey repr. 1836 and 1847.**

"Cowper, priding himself on adhering closely to his original, adhered only in part. . . . By modelling his blank verse on Milton's he achieves inversions, pauses and pomposities which are wholly unlike the smooth and simple rapidity of Homer. This is not to say that there are not excellent passages in Cowper's Homer, nor that the whole work is not a lofty achievement in scholarship and poetry."—*Harold Child in Camb. Hist. Eng. Lit.*

"I hate Cowper's slow, dry, blank verse, so utterly alien to the spirit of the poem, and the minstrel mode of delivery. . . . It is like a prosy, pompous, but unpolished man moving laboriously in a stiff dress of office."—*Sara Coleridge (the only daughter of S. T. Coleridge) in a letter written to her husband,* 1834.

"If Cowper had avoided Pope's obvious faults, he had not the vigour which redeems them. The general effect was cramped and halting. He is so preoccupied with the desire to avoid Pope's excess of ornament that he becomes bald and prosaic."—*Sir Leslie Stephen in the D.N.B.*

\*POPE (ALEXANDER) The Iliad and the Odyssey.(1715.) Repr. *Bohn's Class. Lib.* with Flaxman's designs. Bell, 1902. And in *The Chandos Classics.* Warne. (N.Y., Macmillan, etc.)

"In elevated passages he is powerful, as Homer is powerful, though not in the same way; but in plain narrative, where Homer is still powerful and delightful, Pope, by the inherent fault of his style, is ineffective and out of taste."—*Matthew Arnold, On Translating Homer.*

"Not only did he often miss the meaning of the original, but he followed his predecessors in editions which had no warrant in the Greek. . . . At the same time, others have produced translations but Pope's work is a poem." —*Edward Bensley, Camb. Hist. Eng. Lit.*

"No one will venture to say Pope's *Iliad* has gone, or is likely to go, out of fashion."—*W. J. Courthope in The Works of Pope, Vol. 3, p. 35.*

"And yet . . . Pope is not dethroned. A version, which is in many respects a travesty of the *Iliad*, remains the national version. . . . Pope's *Iliad*, indeed, neither should nor can sink into oblivion. . . . But it is not a satisfactory reflection that, while the standard versions of most other languages approximate more or less closely to the spirit of Homer, that of our own is hopelessly and ostentatiously alien from it."—*Richard Garnett in On Translating Homer (Essays of an Ex-Librarian).*

MURRAY (A. T.) The Iliad. 2 vols. *Loeb Class. Lib.* Heinemann, 1924. (N.Y., Putnam.)

—— The Odyssey. 2 vols. *Loeb Class. Lib.* Heinemann, 1924. (N.Y., Putnam.)

The *Loeb* Homer is in prose. It reads very easily, and the style is less conventional than Lang's.

## The Iliad

DERBY (EDWARD, EARL OF) The Iliad: a blank verse translation. (1865.) Repr. in the *Everyman's Library.* Dent. (N.Y., Dutton.)

"Of all the translations of Homer I prefer Lord Derby's *Iliad* and Philip Worsley's *Odyssey.* Lord Derby preserves something of the dignity of the *Iliad*, which is essential to it. . . ."—*Frederic Harrison in The Choice of Books.*
"Lord Derby's style has very little ornament. . . . He draws near to, though he never reaches, the worst features of the poetic diction of the last (i.e. the eighteenth) century. . . . His version is written in blank verse, and in a slightly conventionalized literary English. It thus comes closest in general characteristics and circumstances to Cowper." At this point the critic quotes a famous passage from the Greek and compares Derby's version of it with Hobbes's, Dryden's, Pope's, Cowper's and Sotheby's. He continues: "If they be compared with each other, and with the original, Lord Derby's is the only one which deserves the name of a translation at all, while it is at least the equal poetically of all but Dryden's. . . . In contrast Lord Derby's version, while not in the

least tame, is simple, stately and exact. It misses nothing
of the slightest importance, and inserts nothing superfluous. . . . In other words, it is a translation of the Greek
and it is comely and sufficient English; and what need
mortals ask for more?"—*Professor Saintsbury in The Life
of Lord Derby.*

\*LANG (ANDREW), WALTER LEAF and ERNEST MYERS.
The Iliad: a prose translation. 1883. Revised,
Macmillan, 1901.

> The artificiality of the style and "tone" of this famous
> version is beginning to date now, and modern ears are
> apt to grow tired of it long before the end.
> "Each (i.e. the *Iliad* and the *Odyssey*) is incomparably
> superior to any of its predecessors in the same line, and
> neither is likely to be superseded as an aid to students."—
> *The Athenæum.*
> "Of the prose translations that of Mr. Andrew Lang and
> his friends is as perfect as a prose translation of verse
> can be. It necessarily loses the movement, the lilt and the
> subtle charm of the verse."—*Frederic Harrison in The
> Choice of Books.*
> "The version which in our day has been most generally
> accepted is undoubtedly the prose of Messrs. Lang,
> Butcher, Leaf and Myers."—*Walter Headlam in the
> preface to A Book of Greek Verse.*

PURVES (JOHN) The Iliad: a prose translation. Edited
with an intro. by Evelyn Abbot. London, Percival,
1891.

> "Quite admirable, and no whit inferior, in its own way,
> to Lang, Leaf and Myers."—*H. MacNaghten, Sunday
> Times, January 29, 1928.*

\*\*WAY (A. S.) The Iliad: a verse translation. Low,
1886. Repr. Macmillan.

> This has been termed a noble version, the charm of
> which is occasionally spoilt by archaic oddities, as, "Onset-

H

yell", "outrage-wild", "forthright", etc. "By far the most spirited and, except Worsley, the most poetical among the recent translators of Homer."—*Richard Garnett in On Translating Homer.*

## The Odyssey

\*BUTCHER (S. H.) and ANDREW LANG. The Odyssey: a prose version. Macmillan, 1879.

> For notes see under the *Iliad* group, under Lang, Leaf and Myers.

COTTERILL (H. B.) The Odyssey. Harrap, 1911.

> An interesting experiment in a line-for-line translation in hexameters.

MACKAIL (J. W.) The Odyssey. 3 vols. Murray, 1912.

> A rendering in quatrains. "The whole of this version is pleasant to read, an easy narrative, following with remarkably little padding or omission the words of the original, couched in beautiful language, sometimes a little exquisite, but always simple and dignified. Though the verse hardly ever sinks to dullness, it does not rise to moments of high inspiration, such as Homer, even in these later books of the *Odyssey*, sometimes attains."—*Class. Rev.,* Vol. 26, *p.* 68.

MORRIS (WILLIAM) The Odyssey. 1887. Repr. Longmans, 1896. (N.Y., Longmans.)

> This translation is couched in archaic diction which is generally considered to have spoilt its effect.

\*\*PALMER (G. H.) The Odyssey: a prose version. Boston, Houghton, 1908. Revised edn., 1921. (English edn., Constable.)

> This work is highly praised in the U.S.A., but does not seem to have excited much attention in England. For readers who are tired of the artificiality of Lang, Leaf

and Myers this may well prove to be the best existing prose version. The more masculine style of this translation is certainly to be preferred, in the compiler's opinion, to the standard English version.

WAY (A. S.) The Odyssey: a verse translation. Macmillan, 1904.

**WORSLEY (P. S.) The Odyssey: a verse translation. Blackwood, 1861.

> Worsley also left an unfinished version of the *Iliad*, which was completed by J. Conington and published by Blackwood in 1865.
>
> "Mr. Worsley, applying the Spenserian stanza . . . has produced a version of the *Odyssey* much the most pleasing of those hitherto produced, and which is delightful to read."—*Matthew Arnold in Last Words on Translating Homer.*
>
> "This masterly translation does all that can be done for the *Odyssey* in the romantic style. The smoothness of the verse, the wonderful closeness to the original, reproduce all of Homer, in music and in meaning, that can be rendered in English verse."—*S. H. Butcher and A. Lang in preface to their version of the Odyssey.*

SUMMARY.—The reader who approaches Homer for the first time may well be overwhelmed by the multitude of translations to choose from and by the variety of opinions to aid him in his choice. I do not think that there is any doubt, however, of the truth of the statement that nobody can afford to neglect the translations of Chapman and Pope. Of the prose versions, those who like the conventional style of "poetic" prose will, of course, like Butcher, Lang, Leaf and Myers; those who like stimulating, unconventional translations will read Samuel Butler's versions; for those who can obtain it, however, Palmer's prose version is highly recommended. Of the modern verse translations, Worsley's and Way's are probably the best.

# HOMERIC HYMNS

*CHAPMAN (GEORGE) Homeric hymns; and, The Epigrams. (1624.) Repr. in 1858; and in 1920 by Chatto and Windus. (N.Y., Scribner.)

>A rough version, it is true; yet dignity and vigour are here too, and Homeric grandeur not infrequent.

EDGAR (JOHN) Homeric hymns: a prose translation. Thim, Edinburgh, 1891.

>An excellent translation, esteemed by Lang.

EVELYN-WHITE (H. G.) Homerica. *Loeb Class. Lib.* Heinemann, 1915. (N.Y., Putnam.)

>Included in the volume which contains the works of Hesiod. "A careful and accurate translation."—*Class. Rev., Vol.* 30, *p.* 16.

**LANG (ANDREW) Homeric hymns: a new prose translation with essays. G. Allen, 1899. (N.Y., Longmans.)

SHELLEY (P. B.) Homeric hymns. (1821.) Repr. O.U.P. edition of Poetical Works, etc., and in a limited edition by the Halcyon Press, 1929.

>"Admirably executed."—*Professor Dowden in The Life of Shelley.*
>
>*See also* Batrachomyomachia.

## HYBRIAS
### (Fl. 31-38 B.C.)
*See* Howe and Harrer (Appendix).

# HYPERIDES
## (4th cent. B.C.)

KENYON (SIR F. G.) The Orations against Athenogenes and Philippides. Bell, 1893. (N.Y., Macmillan.)


# IAMBLICHUS
## (Fl. A.D. 300)

TAYLOR (THOMAS) The Life of Pythagoras. (1818.) Repr. J. M. Watkins, London, 1926. (Point Loma, Cal., Theosophical Publ. Co., 1918. *An abridged version.*)

—— On the mysteries of the Egyptians, Chaldeans and Assyrians. (1821.) Repr., Dobell, 1895.

WILDER (ALEXANDER) Theurgia; or, the Egyptian mysteries. Rider, 1911.


# ÎBYCUS
## (Fl. 540 B.C.)

Poetic fragments. *See* "Lyra Graeca"; and Howe and Harrer (Appendix).


# IGNATIUS, SAINT
## (Fl. A.D. 110)

SRAWLEY (J. H.) Epistles. *Trans. of Christian Lit. Series.* S.P.C.K., 1919. (N.Y., Macmillan.)

*See also* Apostolic Fathers (Appendix).

# IRENAEUS
### (Fl. A.D. 170)

*See* Apostolic Fathers (Appendix).

# ISAEUS
### (Fl. *c.* 400 B.C.)

*FORSTER (E. S.) Speeches. *Loeb Class. Lib.* Heinemann, 1927. (N.Y., Putnam.)

JONES (SIR WM.) Speeches. London, 1779.

# ISOCRATES
### (436–338 B.C.)

BARNES (THOMAS) Archidamus; or, The Councell of Warre. London, 1624.

FREESE (JOHN H.) Orations. Bell, 1894.

> This was the first translation into English of the Orations. "A version at once literal enough to afford a model for students, and readable enough to attract the English reader."—*Class. Rev., Vol. 9, p.* 125.

*NORLIN (GEORGE) Orations: the Greek text with a translation. 3 vols. *Loeb Class. Lib.* Heinemann, 1928. (N.Y., Putnam.) *In progress.*

RICE (JAMES) Panegyric of Isocrates. Kelly, 1898.

WILKINS (GEORGE) Panegyric of Isocrates. Dublin, 1881.

WOODHOUSE (W. J.) De Bigis. Univ. Tut. Pr., 1900.

> *Note:* Sir R. C. Jebb's "Attic Orators" (Macmillan, 2 vols.,
> 1876) contains full and admirable extracts translated from
> Isocrates' masterpieces.

# JOHN DAMASCENE, SAINT

## (A.D. 699-753)

ALLIES (M. H.) Treatise on holy images, to which
is added three sermons on the Assumption.
T. Baker, 1898.

WOODWARD (G. R.) Barlaam and Josaph. *Loeb Class.
Lib.* Heinemann, 1914. (N.Y., Putnam.)

> An Eastern story never before translated into English.
> The eleven apologues contain the story of the caskets
> which reappears in "The Merchant of Venice".
>
> *See also* Apostolic Fathers (Appendix).

# JOSEPHUS

## (A.D. 37-98)

THACKERAY (H. ST. JOHN) Works. 8 vols. *Loeb Class.
Lib.* Heinemann, 1926. (N.Y., Putnam.) *In Progress.*

*WHISTON (WILLIAM) Works.

> This is the standard version and is issued in various
> editions, the best of which is that published by Bell,
> revised by A. R. Shilleto, in 5 volumes; that published
> by Chatto is also good. In the U.S.A., Scribner, Dutton
> and Macmillan all issue good editions.

# JULIAN THE APOSTATE
### (A.D. 331–363)

KING (C. W.) Julian the Emperor, containing Gregory Nazianzen's Two invectives, and Libanius' Monody, with Julian's extant theosophical works. *Bohn's Class. Lib*. Bell, 1848.

WRIGHT (WILMER CAVE) Works. 3 vols. *Loeb Class. Lib*. Heinemann, 1913. (N.Y., Putnam.)

# JUSTIN MARTYR
### (103–165 A.D.)

*See* Apostolic Fathers (Appendix).

# KEBES

*See* Cebes.

# LAMPROCLES
### (Fl. 6th cent. B.C.)

Poetic fragments. *See* "Lyra Graeca" (Appendix).

# LASUS
### (Fl. 650 B.C.)

Poetic fragments. *See* "Lyra Graeca" (Appendix).

# LEONIDAS OF TARENTUM
### (Fl. 3rd cent. B.C.)

WHITALL (JAMES) Poems: a prose trans. *Poets' Trans. Series*. Egoist Pr. 1921.

Poetic fragments. *See also* Greek Anthology (Appendix).

[ 120 ]

# LONGINUS

(Fl. 3rd cent. A.D.)

FYFE (W. HAMILTON) On the sublime. *Loeb Class. Lib.* Heinemann, 1927. (N.Y., Putnam.) *Bound with* Aristotle's "Poetics".

HAVELL (H. S.) Treatise on the sublime. Intro. by Andrew Lang. Macmillan, 1890.

PRICKARD (A. O.) On the sublime. O.U.P., 1906.

*ROBERTS (W. RHYS) On the sublime. Greek text after the Paris MS., with intro., translation and notes. C.U.P., 1899. (N.Y., Macmillan.)

> "The translation has been executed with care and skill, and is more faithful to the original than other English versions. . . . The main defect of this translation is want of verve and also lightness of touch."—*Class. Rev., Vol.* 13, *p.* 403.
>
> *Note:* This famous treatise is now generally attributed by most scholars to an earlier writer than Longinus, probably Dionysius of Halicarnassus, but it will always be known as the work of Longinus.

# LONGUS

(Earlier than the 4th or 5th cent. A.D.)

LOWE (W. D.) Daphnis and Chloe, edited with text, intro., translation and notes. Bell, 1908. (N.Y., Macmillan.)

**MOORE (GEORGE) Daphnis and Chloe. Heinemann, 1925. Repr. in cheaper edn., 1927.

> This is a beautiful piece of work, worthy of being read through in one sitting. It is not conceivable that there will be a better version.

"No version in English reproduces more limpidly the spirit of the original. His book is in itself a work of art."
—*Times Lit. Supp.*

SMITH (ROWLAND) The Pastoral amours of Daphnis and Chloe. *Bohn's Class. Lib.* Bell, 1848.

> Included in a volume which also contains the Greek romances of Heliodorus and Achilles Tatius.

*THORNLEY (GEORGE) Daphnis and Chloe. (1657.) Repr. Chapman and Dodd, in the *Abbey Classics*, 1920. (Boston, Small.)

> There is also an edition of this translation, revised by J. M. Edmonds, in the *Loeb Classical Library*. The translation, on the whole, is couched in English which well suits the pastoral style of the original, and indeed, until George Moore's recent version, was undoubtedly the best.

# LUCIAN

### (Fl. A.D. 150)

**FOWLER (H. W. and F. G.) Works. 4 vols. O.U.P., 1905.

> "Not only correct, but forcible, spirited and natural, with nothing of the conventional translation about it . . . an admirable rendering of him."—*Class. Rev., Vol. 20, p.* 118.

FRANKLIN (THOMAS) Works. 2 vols. London, 1780.

HARMON (A. M.) Works. 8 vols. *Loeb Class. Lib.* Heinemann, 1913–25. (N.Y., Putnam.)

*Hickes (Francis) Certain select dialogues. (1634.) Repr. in *Watergate Library*. Guy Chapman, 1925.

> Of the older translations this is undoubtedly the best. The "True History" was reprinted in 1894 by a private press, and is now very scarce; another edition published in 1927 by the Golden Cockerel Press contained the Greek text, the translation, and an introduction by J. S. Phillimore, together with decorations by R. Gibbings.

Strong (Herbert A.) The Syrian goddess: a translation of Lucian's "De Dea Syria", with a life of Lucian. Constable, 1913.

Williams (H.) Dialogues of the gods. (N.Y., Macmillan; Rev. and enlarged edn., in 2 vols., McKay.)

# LUCILIUS

(148–103 B.C.)

Poetic fragments. *See* Greek Anthology (Appendix).

# LYCOPHRON

(Fl. 250 B.C.)

*Mair (A. W.) The Alexandra. *Loeb Class. Lib.* Heinemann, 1921. (N.Y., Putnam.)

> Bound with the works of Callimachus.

[ 123 ]

Mooney (G. W.) The Alexandra: a blank verse translation. Bell, 1921.

> "As regards the translation, he states that his aim has been 'to give the meaning of the Greek as clearly and simply as possible.' In this he has succeeded admirably." —*E. A. Barber, Class. Rev., Vol.* 36.

Royston (Lord) The Cassandra; or, Alexandra: a verse translation. (Cambridge, 1806.) Repr. London, 1832 and 1859.

## LYSIAS
### (Fl. 4th cent. B.C.)

Gillies (John) Orations. London, 1778.

> The oration against Eratosthenes is reprinted in Howe and Harrer's "Spirit of the Classics". Harper, 1924.

Handy Literal Translations Series. Orations. (N.Y., McKay.)

## MACEDONIUS CONSUL
### (Date uncertain)
*See* Greek Anthology (Appendix).

## MAECIUS
### (Date uncertain)
*See* Greek Anthology (Appendix).

## MARCUS AURELIUS
*See* Aurelius.

# MARK THE DEACON
## (Fl. 397 A.D.)

HILL (G. F.) The Life of Porphyry, Bishop of Gaza.
O.U.P., 1913.


# MAXIMUS TYRIUS
## (Fl. A.D. 130)

TAYLOR (THOMAS) Dissertations. 2 vols. London, 1804.


# MELEAGER
## (Fl. 1st cent. A.D.)

ALDINGTON (RICHARD) The Poems of Meleager of
Gadara. Egoist Press, 1920. (N.Y., Knopf, 1921.
In "Medallions of clay".)

*HEADLAM (WALTER) Fifty poems. Macmillan, 1890.

> "The translations are throughout remarkably literal, and,
> with a few exceptions, good."—*Class. Rev., Vol. 5, p.* 26.

WRIGHT (F. A.) The Complete poems of Meleager of
Gadara. Silas Birch, London, 1922.

> *See also* Greek Anthology (Appendix).


# MENANDER
## (342–291 B.C.)

*ALLINSON (F. C.) Principal fragments. *Loeb Class.
Lib*. Heinemann, 1921. (N.Y., Putnam.)

GRENFELL (B. P.) and A. S. HUNT. *Georgós*, the Geneva
fragment; the text, translation and notes. O.U.P.,
1898.

*POST (L. A.) Three plays: the Girl from Samoa; the
Arbitration; the Shearing of Glycera. Edited and
trans. *Broadway Translations*. Routledge, 1929.
(N.Y., Dutton.)

"UNUS MULTORUM" i.e. Pomeroy (James Spencer,
6th Viscount Harberton) Lately discovered fragments of Menander. Edited with English version,
rev. text, notes, etc., J. Parker, Oxford, 1909.


## MIMNERMUS
(6th cent. B.C.)

*See* Howe and Harrer; and Symonds (Appendix).


## MONUMENTUM ANCYRANUM

*See* "Res Gestae divi Augustae" (Appendix).


## MOSCHUS
(Fl. 150 B.C.)

*See* Theocritus.


## MUSAEUS
(Fl. 500 B.C.)

CHAPMAN (GEORGE) Hero and Leander (1629). Repr
Chatto and Windus, 1920.

*See* below under Marlowe.

[ 126 ]

FAWKES (FRANCIS) Hero and Leander. London, 1760.

> This is the best of the many eighteenth-century versions of the poem. There was one by "E.B.G.", published in 1773, and another by G. Bally, published in 1747.

MARLOWE (CHRISTOPHER) Hero and Leander (1598). Repr. Newnes, 1905; Chatto and Windus; O.U.P., etc.

> Marlowe "translated" the first two sestiads only; the remainder of the poem was completed by Chapman. The work purports to be a translation but in reality, save for the plot, the poem is almost entirely original.

*SIKES (E. E.) Hero and Leander, translated into rhyming verse. Methuen, 1920.

## MYRTIS
(Date uncertain)
Poetic fragments. *See* "Lyra Graeca" (Appendix).

## NEMESIUS
(Fl. A.D. 400)

WITHER (GEORGE) The Nature of man. London, 1636.

## NICARCHUS
(Fl. 2nd cent. A.D.)
Poetic fragments. *See* Greek Anthology (Appendix).

# NICOLAUS OF DAMASCUS

(b. 64 B.C.)

HALL (CLAYTON M.) Life of Augustus. (*Smith Coll. Class. Studies.* Northampton, Mass., 1923.)

"A historical commentary embodying a translation."


# NICOMACHUS OF GERASA

(Fl. A.D. 100)

D'OOGE (M. L.) Introduction to arithmetic. (*Univ. of Michigan Studies*, N.Y., Macmillan, 1926.)


# NUMENIUS OF APAMEIA

(Fl. A.D. 160)

GUTHRIE (K. S.) Works, biography, sources, etc. A parallel version in Greek and English. Bell, 1917. (Grantwood, N.J., 1917.)


# "OLD OLIGARCH"

(Fl. 5th cent. B.C.)

BROOKS (FRANCIS) An Athenian critic of Athenian democracy. D. Nutt, 1912.

A translation of "De Republica Atheniensium", often ascribed to Xenophon.

PETCH (J. A.) Old Oligarch: being the constitution of the Athenians, ascribed to Xenophon. Blackwell, 1926.

# OLYMPIA

(Date uncertain)

Poetic Fragments. *See* "Lyra Graeca" (Appendix.)

# ONASANDER

(Fl. A.D. 50)

ILLINOIS GREEK CLUB. The General. *Loeb Class. Lib.*
Heinemann, 1923. (N.Y., Putnam.)

> Included in the volume which contains the works of
> Aeneas Tacticus.

WHYTEBORNE (PETER) Onosandro Platonico, of the
Generall Captaine and of his Office. London, 1563.

# OPPIAN

(Fl. A.D. 180)

DRAPER and JONES. Halieuticks; of the nature of fishes
and fishing of the ancients. Oxford, 1722.

*MAIR (A. W.) Cynegetica and Halieutica: a prose
translation. *Loeb Class. Lib.* Heinemann, 1928.
(N.Y., Putnam.)

MAWER (JOHN) First book of Cynegetics; or, Poem of
hunting, translated into English verse. York, 1736.

# ORPHEUS

(Before the time of Homer)

TAYLOR (THOMAS) Mystical institutions; or, Hymns of
Orpheus. (Chiswick, 1787.) Rev. edn. 1824. Repr.,
Dobell, 1896.

# PALATINE ANTHOLOGY
*See* Greek Anthology (Appendix).

# PALLADAS OF ALEXANDRIA
(Date uncertain)

Poetic fragments. *See* Greek Anthology (Appendix).

# PALLADIUS
(Fl. A.D. 400)

CLARKE (W. K. LOWTHER) Lausiac history. S.P.C.K., 1918. (N.Y., Macmillan.)

MOORE (HERBERT) Dialogue concerning the life of St. Chrysostom. S.P.C.K., 1921. (N.Y., Macmillan.)

# PARTHENIUS
(Fl. 50 B.C.)

GASELEE (STEPHEN) Love romance. *Loeb Class. Lib.* Heinemann, 1924. (N.Y., Putnam.)

> Included in the volume which also contains "Daphnis and Chloe".

# PAUL THE SILENTIARY
(Date uncertain)

Poetic fragments. *See* Greek Anthology (Appendix).

Over 100 poems by this author are included in the Palatine Anthology.

# PAUSANIAS

(Fl. A.D. 150)

**FRAZER (SIR J. G.) Description of Greece. 6 vols
Macmillan, 1898.

> This is the standard work of reference and has a monu-
> mental commentary.

*JONES (W. H. S.) and H. A. ORMEROD. Description of
Greece. 5 vols. *Loeb Class. Lib.* Heinemann, 1918.
(N.Y., Putnam.)

> This is considered the best ordinary edition of Pausanius,
> and superior to that in *Bohn's Classical Library.*

VERRALL (MARGARET DE G.) Attica: mythology and
monuments of ancient Athens; being a translation
of a portion of the "Attica" of Pausanius. Macmillan, 1890.


# PHALARIS

(Fl. 570 B.C.)

FRANCKLIN (T.) Epistles. London, 1749.


# PHILAGRIUS

*See* Hierocles.


# PHILIPPUS OF THESSALONICA

(Fl. A.D. 100)

Poetic fragments. *See* Greek Anthology (Appendix).

[ 131 ]

# PHILODEMUS

## (1st cent. B.C.)

HUBBELL (HARRY M.) Rhetorica: a trans. and a commentary. (Translations of the Connecticut Academy of Arts and Sciences. Vol. 23, pp. 243–382.) Yale Univ. Press, New Haven, Conn., 1920.

> "The title of Dr. Hubbell's work is doubly misleading. In the ordinary sense of the word what he gives is neither a translation nor a commentary. An introductory essay and bibliography are followed by an abridged paraphrase of the text of Philodemus' two works on rhetoric as presented by Sudhaus in the three Teubner volumes."— *J. L. Stock, Class. Rev., Vol. 38, p. 32.*

Poetic fragments. *See* Greek Anthology (Appendix).


# PHILO JUDAEUS

*See* Latin Section.


# PHILOSTORGIUS

## (Fl. A.D. 358)

WALFORD (EDWARD) Ecclesiastical history. *Bohn's Eccles. Lib.* Bell, 1855.

> Included in the volume which also contains the history of Sozomen.

# PHILOSTRATUS

(b. A.D. 182)

CONYBEARE (F. C.) Apollonius of Tyana. 2 vols. *Loeb Class. Lib.* Heinemann, 1912. (N.Y., Putnam.)

EELLS (CHAS. P.) Life and Times of Apollonius of Tyana. (*Univ. Ser. of Lang. and Lit.*, Vol. 2, No. 1.) Stamford Univ., Cal. 1923.

*PHILLIMORE (J.S.) In honour of Apollonius of Tyana. 2 vols. O.U.P., 1912.

> "A very brilliant piece of work."—*A. W. Pickard, The Year's Work in Class. Studies.*

WRIGHT (W. C.) Lives of the Sophists. *Loeb. Class. Lib.* Heinemann, 1922. (N.Y., Putnam.)

> "Philostratus' gallery of little sketches of those marvellous verbal executants makes the liveliest reading in the Greek, but this translation is flat and colourless; the nuances are frequently missed, the wit disappears. . . ." —*J. S. Phillimore, Class. Rev., Vol. 38, p. 76.*


# PHOCYLIDES

(Fl. 537 B.C.)

GOODWIN (H. D.) Poem of admonition. Intro. and commentaries by J. B. Feuling. Andover, Mass., 1879.

HART (J.) Poem of admonition. London, 1744.

HEWETT (W.) The Preceptive poem of Phocylides, trans. into English verse. Watford, 1840.

## PHOTIUS
### (Patriarch of Constantinople, d. A.D. 891)

FREESE (J. H.) The Library of Photius. *Trans. of Christian Lit. Series.* S.P.C.K., 1920. (N.Y., Macmillan.)

WALFORD (EDWARD) The Ecclesiastical history of Philostorgius as epitomized by Photius. *Bohn's Ecclesiastical Lib.* Bell, 1855.

## PINDAR
### (522–448 B.C.)

BARING (T. C.) Epinician odes and fragments in English rhymed verse. London, 1875.

BILLSON (C. J.) The Olympian and Pythian Odes, with an introduction and a trans. into English verse. Stratford-on-Avon. Blackwell, 1929.

> An expensive, limited edition. The translation is a fine piece of work and it is hoped that it may eventually be made available to a larger public in an ordinary edition.

COWLEY (ABRAHAM) Pindarique odes. (1656.) Repr. O.U.P., etc.

> These odes were more in the nature of paraphrases than translations, as a perusal of Cowley's preface will show. Their vigour and strength, however, have won them the

praise of many great critics, including Dryden. Furthermore, in Cowley's opinion a paraphrase of Pindar is the nearest—if not the only—approach in English to the original. He said that "if a man should undertake to translate Pindar word for word, it would be thought that one madman had translated another."

MOBERLEY (GEORGE) *Bishop of Salisbury.* The Odes, trans. into English metre. Winchester, 1876.

*MOORE (ABRAHAM) The Odes: a metrical translation. (1822.) Repr. in *Bohn's Class. Lib.* Bell, 1868. (N.Y., Macmillan; also privately printed by N. A. Dole.)

> Included in a volume which also contains a literal prose version of Pindar by D. W. Turner. "Moore's translation is incomparably the best, both in scholarship and in literary power."—*F. D. Morice.*

MORICE (F. D.) The Olympian and Pythian Odes. (1876.) Repr. Percival, 1893. (Phil., Lippincott.)

**MYERS (ERNEST) The Extant odes; including thirty-one early fragments, trans. into prose. Macmillan, 1874, 1892.

> This version was highly praised by Frederic Harrison. It was, he thought, as perfect a translation as any prose version of a poet can be.

PALEY (F. A.) The Odes: a prose translation. Williams and Norgate, 1868.

**SANDYS (SIR J. E.) The Odes: a prose translation. *Loeb Class. Lib.* Heinemann, 1915. (N.Y., Putnam.)

> "Scholarly and dignified."—*Class. Rev., Vol.* 31, *p.* 98.

TURNER (D. W.) The Odes: literally translated into English prose, with a metrical version by A. MOORE. *Bohn's Class. Lib.* Bell, 1868.

> This edition is chiefly valuable for the reprint of Moore's version, which is noted above.

*WAY (A. S.) The Odes: translated into English verse. Macmillan, 1922.

# PLATO

### (427–347 B.C.)

CARY (H.) and others. Works: a new and literal version. 6 vols. *Bohn's Class. Lib.* Bell, 1848.

> Unequal, as such an edition must necessarily be. Many of the dialogues are made unforgivably dull. Cary's translation of the "Crito" dialogue was reprinted in 1926 by Harper.

*CHURCH (F. J.) The Trial and death of Socrates: being the Euthyphron, Apology, Crito and Phaedo. *Golden Treasury Series.* Macmillan, 1890. (N.Y., Macmillan; and Burt.)

EVERYMAN'S LIBRARY. Dialogues. 2 vols. Dent, 1910. (N.Y., Dutton.)

> *Contents*:—Five dialogues bearing on poetic inspiration: Ion and the Symposium, trans. by P. B. Shelley (1820); the Meno, trans. by Floyer Sydenham (1773); the Phaedo, trans. by Henry Cary (1848); the Phaedrus, trans. by J. Wright (1840). The second volume contains a reprint of the "Republic", translated by H. Spens (1763).

**\*\*JOWETT (BENJAMIN)** The Dialogues: trans. with analysis and introductions. 5 vols. O.U.P., 1892. (N.Y., O.U.P.; Bigelow, Brown and Co.; and Scribner.)

> Messrs. Scribners have also published an excellent selection of these great dialogues in a series entitled the *Modern Student's Library of Philosophy.*
> "All these three great works [i.e. Jowett's translations of Plato, Thucydides and the "Politics" of Aristotle] are justly recognized as masterpieces of English, and his rendering of Plato in particular, with its admirably written introductions, has, in fact, made Plato an English classic."— *Sir J. E. Sandys's Hist. of Class. Scholarship, Vol.* 3, *p.* 419.
> The above note is typical of most of the opinions of scholars and critics on Jowett's famous translation. The late J. S. Phillimore, however, in a pamphlet entitled "On Translations and Translation", placed himself in a minority by writing the following: "How falsified is Plato in Jowett's much-belauded version! How inadequate was Jowett to apprehend, much more to reproduce, even with Swinburne's prompting, the finesse, the slyness, the deftness of his author."

**\*LOEB CLASSICAL LIBRARY.** Works. 10 vols. Heinemann, 1914–1926. (N.Y., Putnam.)

> *Contents:*—Euthyphro, Apology, Crito, Phaedo, Phaedrus, trans. by H. N. Fowler; the Laws, 2 vols., by R. G. Bury; the Republic, by Paul Shorey; Theaetetus and Sophist, by H. N. Fowler; Cratylus, Parmenides, Philebus and Politicus, by H. N. Fowler; Alcibiades, Amatores, Charmides, Ion, by W. R. M. Lamb.
> The complete works of Plato are not yet issued in this series, but those that have been reviewed have been praised for their uniform excellence. The dialogues by H. N. Fowler are particularly noteworthy for their easy, flowing rendering.

TAYLOR (A. E.) Timæus and Critias. Methuen, 1930.

> "The translation will be valued by all students of Plato. [There is] general agreement in regard to the masterly manner in which the whole work has been done."— *G. Dawes Hicks in the Hibbert Journal.*

### The Republic

*DAVIES (J. L.) and D. J. VAUGHAN. The Republic. *Golden Treasury Series.* Macmillan, 1866. (N.Y., Macmillan; and Burt.)

SPENS (HARRY) The Republic. (1763.) Repr. *Everyman's Library.* Dent, 1906. (N.Y., Dutton.)

> "On the whole Spens's version should not be lightly esteemed. It is clearly the work of a scholar and a man of considerable literary ability."—*R. Garnett.*
> *Note:* Jowett's translation of the *Republic* is also available in cheaper form than the collected edition noted above.

### The Symposium

*BIRRELL (FRANCIS) and SHANE LESLIE. The Symposium; or, Banquet. Fortune Press, 1927.

> A smooth and scholarly version, beautifully printed and produced. Previously issued in similar *format* by the Nonesuch Press.

SHELLEY (PERCY B.) The Banquet; or, The Symposium. (1818.) Repr. *Everyman's Library.* Dent, 1910. (N.Y., Dutton.)

> This famous translation is reprinted with four other dialogues. As in all of Shelley's translations the beauty of the language compensates for the departures from the original. Jowett's translation of the *Symposium* is also issued in cheaper form.

POST (L. A.) Three epistles: intro., trans. and notes. O.U.P., 1926.

> "In the main an accurate and readable version."—*Class. Rev., Vol.* 40, *p.* 123.

SHELLEY (PERCY B.) Epigrams of Plato. Repr. in all collected editions.

> *See also* in volumes of the Greek Anthology.

> SUMMARY.—Jowett's translation is known all over the world as a classic in itself. There are critics, the late Mr. Phillimore for example, who think it much over-praised, but it is likely to maintain its position for many decades to come. The *Loeb* version is admirable, particularly the volumes for which H. N. Fowler is responsible; the cheap edition of Davies and Vaughan's "*Republic*" in the *Golden Treasury Series* is also strongly recommended. It is difficult to procure Jowett's five-volume edition now, but fortunately the O.U.P. have issued the Socratic dialogues and the "*Republic*" in single volumes at low prices, thus making easily accessible the finest of these incomparable literary entertainments.

# PLOTINUS

### (A.D. 203–262)

*GUTHRIE (K. S.) Complete works, with biography by Porphyry, commentaries, etc. 4 vols. (N.Y., Platonist Press, 1918, and Chicago, Open Court Publ. Co.)

*McKenna (Stephen) Ethical treatises and Enneads. Medici Society, 1917. (Boston, Medici Society.) *In progress.*

> A beautiful but very expensive edition.
> The sixth treatise of the first Ennead entitled "On the Beautiful" is published also in a cheaper form by Blackwells.
> "His translation is always lucid and pleasant to read. . . . It must be clearly stated that this gigantic labour of love deserves the most respectful recognition by all scholars."
> —*W. R. Inge in Class. Rev., Vol. 36, p. 27.*

Taylor (Thomas) Select works. (1794.) Repr. *Bohn's Class. Lib.* Bell, 1848. (N.Y., an edn. edited by G. R. S. Read, and Harcourt.)

# PLUTARCH

## (A.D. 46–120)

### *The Lives*

*Clough (A. H.) The Parallel lives. (1859.) Repr. *Everyman's Library.* 3 vols. Dent, 1910. (N.Y., Dutton; Burt; and Bigelow, Brown and Co.)

> This translation is really a revision of a very indifferent work published in 1683 and known as Dryden's translation. Dryden, however, contributed only a life of Plutarch and a preface. Of the original translation J. and W. Langhorne write: "The diversities of style were not the greatest fault of this strange translation. It was full of the grossest errors. Ignorance on the one hand and hastiness or negligence on the other, had filled it with absurdities and inaccuracies. . . . The language in general was insupportably tame, and embarrassed." Professor Perrin in his preface to the *Loeb* version said of Clough's revision: that it "is probably the best extant English version of the Lives".

LANGHORNE (JOHN and WILLIAM) The Lives. (1770.) Repr. *Chandos Classics*. Warne, 1927. (N.Y., Scribner.)

> "Compared with North's spirited version, it is rather dull and pedantic."—*B. Perrin.*

**NORTH (SIR THOMAS) The Lives of the noble Grecians and Romans, compared together by Plutarke, done into English from the French of Amyot. (1579.) Repr. *Temple Classics*. 9 vols. Dent, 1898–9. (N.Y., Dutton.)

> A limited edition was also published in 1928 by Blackwell, at the Shakespeare Head Press, Oxford, in eight volumes.
> ". . . North's incomparable prose . . . North's achievement in narrative prose is only less signal than Shakespeare's in dramatic verse. I doubt if there are many pages which may rank with the last of North's Antonius in the prose of any language. . . . Of good English prose there is much, but of the world's greatest books in great English prose there are not many. Here is one, worthy to stand with Malory's *Morte D'Arthur* on either side the English Bible."—*George Wyndham, Essays in Romantic Literature.*
> "The most famous and perhaps the best of Elizabethan translations. . . . It is not Plutarch. In many respects it is Plutarch's antithesis. North composed a new masterpiece upon Plutarch's theme. He saw Plutarch through Amyot's eye, and the result is neither Amyot nor Plutarch. North, though he knew little of the classics, was a master of noble English. . . . He played upon English prose as upon an organ, whose every stop he controls with an easy confidence. . . . There are few who, were the choice given them, would not rather read Plutarch in the noble English of North, than in the restrained and sometimes inexpressive Greek of Plutarch."—*Charles Whibley, Camb. Hist. Eng. Lit., Vol. 4, pp. 9–12.*

\*PERRIN (B.) Parallel lives. 11 vols. *Loeb Class. Lib.* Heinemann, 1916–1926. (N.Y., Putnam.)

> A good version, coming probably between North's and Clough's in order of merit.
> "He has been content to render his author in plain and simple English prose, which is very easy and very pleasing to read."—*Class. Rev., Vol.* 30, *p.* 89.

> "The translation is faithful. This new version shows, I think, a certain lack of that appreciation for the less obvious idioms of English which some scholars seem to lose in acquiring an ancient language."—*J. M. Edmonds in The Year's Work in Class. Studies,* 1916.

STEWART (A.) and GEORGE LONG. The Lives. 4 vols. *Bohn's Popular Lib.* Bell, 1914. (N.Y., Harcourt.)

## *The Moralia*

BABBITT (F. C.) Moralia. 14 vols. *Loeb Class. Lib.* Heinemann, 1927. (N.Y., Putnam.) *In Progress.*

\*HOLLAND (PHILEMON) Morals (1603); and, Romane Questions (1603). The "Morals" has been reprinted in *Everyman's Library.* Dent, 1912. (N.Y., Dutton.)

> *Romane Questions* was re-issued in 1892, under the editorship of F. B. Jevons, by Nutt.
> "Holland's Pliny and Plutarch are almost unique among translations. They not only reproduce their originals with sufficient accuracy to be useful, but they give them a fresh and a genuine literary value. They contain an extraordinary wealth of English and a quaint felicity of phrase."
> —*W. Warde Fowler, Class. Rev., Vol.* 7, *p.* 322.

*The Roman Questions*

\*HOLLAND (PHILEMON) The Romane Questions. (1603.) Repr. 1892, D. Nutt.

ROSE (H. J.) Roman Questions: a new translation, with essays and comm. O.U.P., 1924.

*Miscellaneous Works*

TUCKER (G.) and A. O. PRICKARD. Select essays. 2 vols. O.U.P., 1913–1918.

# POLYAENUS
(Fl. A.D. 150)

SHEPHERD (R.) Stratagems of war. London, 1793.

# POLYBIUS
(205–123 B.C.)

HAMPTON (JAMES) The General history of Polybius, 4 vols. London, 1772.

This translation is recommended by Professor B. Wendell.

\*PATON (W. R.) The History of Polybius. 6 vols. *Loeb Class. Lib.* Heinemann, 1922–27. (N.Y., Putnam.)

A good piece of work which has earned the praise of scholarly critics.

SHUCKBURGH (EVELYN S.) The Histories of Polybius. 2 vols. Macmillan, 1889. (N.Y., Macmillan.)

# POLYCARP, SAINT

(b. A.D. 70)

Epistles. *See* Apostolic Fathers (Appendix).


# POLYMNASTUS

(Fl. 650 B.C.)

Poetic fragments. *See* "Lyra Graeca" (Appendix).


# PORPHYRY

(b. A.D. 233)

TAYLOR (THOMAS) Select works, containing 4 books
on abstinence from animal food; treatise on the
Homeric cave of the nymphs; and Auxiliaries to
the perception of intelligible natures. London,
1823.


# POSEIDIPPUS

(Fl. 3rd cent. B.C.)

STORER (EDWARD) Poems. Egoist Press, 1920.

*See also* Greek Anthology (Appendix).


# PROCLUS

(A.D. 412–485)

GUTHRIE (K. S.) Life, hymns and works. (N.Y.,
Platonist Press.)

TAYLOR (THOMAS) On the theology of Plato, etc., 8 vols. London, 1792–1833.

Five hymns of Proclus are translated in a metrical version by Thomas Taylor in a work published in 1793 which also included the treatise "On the Gods" by Sallust.

## PROCOPIUS
### (Fl. A.D. 500)

DEWING (H. B.) History of the wars. 7 vols. *Loeb Class. Lib.* Heinemann, 1914–24. (N.Y., Putnam.)

HOLCROFT (SIR HENRY) History of the warres of the Emperour Justinian. London, 1653.

"It is a fine piece of work and worthy of study."—*G. W. Butterworth, Class. Rev., Vol.* 31, *p.* 53.

## PRODICUS
### (Fl. 400 B.C.)

*CLARK (R. THOMSON) The Choice of Heracles. Routledge, 1909. (N.Y., Dutton.)

Included in the volume containing the *Characters* of Theophrastus.

LOWTH (BISHOP) The Choice of Heracles. Published in Roach's "Beauties of the Poets", 1794.

## PSELLUS
### (Fl. A.D. 860)

COLLISSON (MARCUS) Dialogue on the operation of Daemons. J. Tegg. Sydney, 1843.

# PTOLEMY

(Claudius Ptolemaeus. Fl. A.D. 160)

## *Tetra biblos.*

ASHMEAD (J. M.) Tetra biblos, newly trans. from the Greek paraphrase of Proclus. London, 1822. (Repr. Foulsham, 1917.)

WILSON (JAMES) The Tetra biblos; or, Quadripartite of Ptolemy, being four books relative to the starry influences. London, 1828.

### *Geography*

MCCRINDLE (J. W.) Ancient India as described by Ptolemy; being a trans. of the chapters which describe India and Eastern Asia in the treatise on geography; with intro., commentary, notes, etc. Thacker. Calcutta, 1885.

# PTOLEMY PHILADELPHUS

(Fl. 308–247 B.C.)

GRENFELL (B. P.) Revenue laws. Edited from the Greek papyrus in the Bodleian Library with trans., commentary, etc. Intro. by J. P. Mahaffy. O.U.P., 1896.

# PYTHAGORAS

(582–500 B.C.)

*GUTHRIE (K. S.) Golden verses. (N.Y., Platonist Press.)

POVEY (JOHN) Golden verses. London, 1886.

# QUINTUS SMYRNAEUS
### (Fl. 4th cent. A.D.)

WAY (A. S.) The Fall of Troy: a verse translation.
*Loeb Class. Lib.* Heinemann, 1913. (N.Y., Putnam.)


# RUFINUS
### (Date uncertain)

Poetic fragments. *See* Greek Anthology (Appendix).


# SACADAS
### (Fl. 580 B.C.)

Poetic fragments. *See* "Lyra Graeca" (Appendix).


# SALLUSTIUS THE PLATONIST
### (Fl. A.D. 360)

MURRAY (GILBERT) On the gods and the universe.

> This translation is contained in "Five stages of Greek religion", a revised edition of which was published by the O.U.P. in 1925.

NOCK (A. D.) Concerning the gods and the universe. Edited with prolegomena and a translation. C.U.P., 1926.

TAYLOR (THOMAS) Sallust on the gods and the world; and, The Pythagoric sentences of Demophilus, etc. London, 1793.

# SAPPHO

## (7th cent. B.C.)

ARNOLD (SIR EDWIN) The Poets of Greece. Cassell, 1869.

> This volume contains some fine translations of Sappho, together with a critical and historical life of the poetess. Many of Arnold's most successful renderings are included in Cox's *The Poems of Sappho*, which is noted below.

CARMAN (BLISS) Sappho; one hundred lyrics. Chatto and Windus, 1910.

> This Canadian poet has attempted to rewrite from the fragments one hundred lost poems.

*COX (E. M.) The Poems of Sappho, with historical and critical notes, a translation and a bibliography. Williams and Norgate, 1924. (N.Y., Scribner.)

> In addition to renderings in prose and verse by the author, this volume contains a selection of the most famous renderings, including those of J. A. Symonds and Sir Edwin Arnold.

*EDMONDS (J. M.) The Poems of Sappho: a prose translation. *Loeb. Class. Lib.* Heinemann, 1922. (N.Y., Putnam.)

> This rendering is included in the collection entitled "Lyra Graeca".

FAWKES (FRANCIS) Poems. (1760.) Repr. in Chalmers's *English Poets*, 1820, and by Valpy in 1832.

MILLER (MARION M.) and D. ROBINSON. The Songs of
Sappho. Maxwelton Co., Lexington, Kentucky,
1926.

> Contains a revised text, a prose translation, notes and
> a translation into rhymed verse (English sapphics) by
> Dr. Miller, whose translation of the "Hymn to Aphrodite"
> is thought by some scholars to be "unquestionably the
> best in our language".

ROBINSON (DAVIDSON) Sappho and her influence.
Harrap, 1924.

> This volume in *Our debt to Greece and Rome Series*
> contains in quotation some of the happiest translations
> of Sappho by various authors.

SYMONDS (J. A.) Translations of Sappho.

> These do not appear to have been included in Symonds's
> volumes of verse, but a few fragments and the "Hymn to
> Aphrodite" will be found in his *Studies in the Greek poets*
> (A. & C. Black, 1920). The latter is also reprinted in
> Howe and Harrer's *Spirit of the Classics*. (See appendix
> of collected translations.)

WAY (A. S.) Sappho and the Vigil of Venus, trans.
into verse. Macmillan, 1920.

**WHARTON (H. T.) Sappho: text, memoir, selected
renderings and literal translation. Simpkin
Marshall, 1885. Repr. Lane, 1895. (N.Y., Brentano
and Lane: i.e. Wood, Mead and Co.)

> The selected renderings are by A. Philips (1711), Merivale,
> Professor Palgrave, Sir R. F. Burton and J. A. Symonds.

> SUMMARY.—The most successful renderings of Sappho
> are generally thought to be those by Sir Edwin Arnold

and J. A. Symonds. Wharton's volume has such a wide selection of translations that it is one of the best for the general reader, and is strongly recommended. Cox's volume is also very good. The American edition of this is a limited edition de luxe.

## SIMONIDES OF CEOS

### (556–468 B.C.)

SCHOMBERG (ALEXANDER C.) Cornelius Scriblerus Nothus, Pseud. An Ode on the present state of English poetry . . . to which is added a translation of a fragment of Simonides. Oxford, 1779.

> See also Greek Anthology, "Lyra Graeca", and Howe and Harrer (Appendix).

## SOCRATES

### (Surnamed "Scholasticus", b. A.D. 379)

ANONYMOUS. Ecclesiastical history from A.D. 305 to 445 *Bohn's Eccles. Lib.* Bell.

> See also Apostolic Fathers (Appendix).

## SOLON

### (Fl. 638 B.C.)

FREEMAN (KATHLEEN) The Work and life of Solon; with a trans. of his poems. O.U.P., 1926.

LINFORTH (I. M.) Poems: text, prose trans. and commentary. Univ. of Chicago Pr., 1919.

> Fragments of Solon's poems will be found translated, with text, in Linforth's *Solon the Athenian*, Univ. of Cal., 1919.

## SOPHOCLES
### (496–406 B.C.)

*Two or more Plays:*

*CAMPBELL (L.) Plays: a verse translation. (1883.) Repr. rev. edn., in *The World's Classics*. O.U.P., 1906.

> "Professor Lewis Campbell's translation of Sophocles is most elegant and, with the accuracy of a scholar, gives us something of the grace and lyric charm of Sophocles."— *Frederic Harrison in The Choice of Books.*

COLERIDGE (E. P.) Tragedies: a prose translation. *Bohn's Class. Lib.* Bell, 1893.

> This is considered to be one of the best of the literal versions of Sophocles.

FRANCKLIN (THOMAS) Plays: a verse translation. (1759.) Repr. in *Morley's Universal Library*. Routledge, 1886. (N.Y., Dutton.)

**JEBB (SIR R. C.) Plays and fragments, with critical notes, commentary and trans. into English prose. 10 vols. C.U.P., 1904. (N.Y., Macmillan.)

> This is a monumental work, but its appeal is mainly to scholars. It must for a long time remain the greatest translation in prose.

[ 151 ]

PHILLIMORE (J. S.) Works: trans. into verse and explained. Allen and Unwin, 1902.

PLUMPTRE (EDWARD H.) Plays: a verse translation. (1865.) Repr. 1908, New Univ. Library, Routledge. (N.Y., Dutton; Heath; and Phil., McKay.)

Plumptre's "complete versions of Aeschylus and Sophocles . . . are the only means by which the English reader is enabled to appreciate the delicate variations of metre in the dramatic scenes."—*Written in 1898, by R. G. Moulton in The Ancient Classical Drama.*

STORR (F.) Plays: a blank verse translation. 2 vols. *Loeb Class. Lib.* Heinemann, 1912. (N.Y., Putnam.)

"It maintains a high level of excellence as translations go. His blank verse, though it rarely rouses our enthusiasm, and is, indeed, occasionally monotonous, never falls below a good level."—*Class. Rev., Vol. 27, p. 106.*

WAY (A. S.) Plays: a verse translation. Macmillan. 1909–1914. (N.Y., Macmillan.)

WHITELAW (ROBERT) The Plays: trans. into English verse. Rivingtons, 1883. Repr., 1897.

The *Antigone* was reprinted in 1927 by the O.U.P.

YOUNG (SIR GEORGE) Four dramas: trans. into English verse. Bell, 1888. Repr. *Everyman's Library*, 1906. (N.Y., Dutton.)

## *Single Plays:*

TREVELYAN (R. C.) Ajax: a verse translation. Allen and Unwin, 1919.

TREVELYAN (R.C.) Antigone: a verse translation. Univ. Liverpool Press, 1924.

*PALMER (G. H.) The Antigone: a verse trans. (Boston, Houghton, 1899.)

WALKER (R. J.) The Ichneutae: notes, text and translation. Burns and Oates, 1919.

> This work was discovered in Egypt in 1907, and is attributed by the translator to Sophocles.

MORSHEAD (E. D. A.) Oedipus King. Macmillan, 1885.

> "Mr. E. D. A. Morshead has been as successful with the Oedipus King of Sophocles as with the Trilogy of Aeschylus."—*Frederic Harrison in The Choice of Books.*

MURRAY (GILBERT) Oedipus King of Thebes: a verse translation. Allen and Unwin, 1911.

*SHEPPARD (J. T.) Oedipus Tyrannus: a verse translation. C.U.P., 1920. (N.Y., Macmillan.)

> "A work of consummate scholarship. The translation, though admirable on the whole, . . . contains some ugly lines: 'pitying not such a petitioning', etc."—*Gilbert Norwood, Class. Rev., Vol. 3, p. 36.*

# SOZOMEN

### (Fl. A.D. 400)

WALFORD (EDWARD) Ecclesiastical history, A.D. 324–440, and the Ecclesiastical history of Philostorgius. *Bohn's Eccles. Lib.* Bell, 1855.

> *See also* Apostolic Fathers (Appendix).

# STESICHORUS

## (632–552 B.C.)

Poetic Fragments. *See* "Lyra Graeca" (Appendix).


# STRABO

## (60 B.C.–A.D. 24)

*FALCONER (W.) and H. C. HAMILTON. Geography. 3 vols. *Bohn's Class. Lib.* Bell, 1854.

JONES (H. L.) Geography. 8 vols. *Loeb Class. Lib.* Heinemann, 1917. (N.Y., Putnam.)

LEAF (W.) On the Troad, Book XIII. Edit. and trans. C.U.P.


# SYNESIUS OF CYRENE

## (Fl. A.D. 390)

BROWNING (E. B.) Hymns. 1842.

> Translated in an article on the Greek Christian poets published in the "Athenæum" in 1842. This article will be found reprinted in the O.U.P. edition of Mrs. Browning's works.

CHATFIELD (A. W.) Lord Jesus, think on me. 1876.

> This well-known translation is the tenth hymn in "Hymns Ancient and Modern".

FITZGERALD (AUGUSTINE) Essays and hymns, including the address to the Emperor Arcadius and the Political speeches: trans., with intro. and notes. 2 vols. O.U.P., 1930.

—— Letters, trans. with intro. and notes. O.U.P., 1926.

## TATIANUS

(Fl. 2nd cent. A.D.)

*See* Apostolic Fathers (Appendix).

## TELESILLA

(Fl. 510 B.C.)

Poetic fragments. *See* "Lyra Graeca" (Appendix).

## TERPANDER

(Fl. 700 B.C.)

Poetic fragments. *See* "Lyra Graeca" (Appendix).

## THALES

(Fl. 650 B.C.)

Poetic fragments. *See* "Lyra Graeca" (Appendix).

# THEOCRITUS

### (Fl. 280 B.C.)

*Under this heading will also be found the works of Bion (fl. 100 B.C.) and Moschus (fl. 150 B.C.). These three writers are known as the "Greek Bucolic Poets" and their works are usually grouped together in one volume.*

ANONYMOUS. Sixe idillia; that is, sixe small, or petty poems, or aeglogues chosen out of the right famous Sicilian poet Theocritus, and translated into English verse. (1588.) Repr. Duckworth, 1922.

> The 1922 reprint of this work is a limited edition de luxe, but the poems are also included in Vol. 8 of Arber's "English garner" (1896); and in "Some longer Elizabethan poems", edited by A. H. Bullen (1903). There is no doubt that these "idillia" have been far luckier than they deserve in being so worthily and frequently reprinted; yet they read prettily enough, and are by no means without grace.

ARNOLD (SIR EDWIN) The Poets of Greece. Cassell, 1869.

> This volume contains some very beautiful and highly praised translations of Theocritus.

BANKS (J.) The Idylls of Theocritus, Bion and Moschus, and the War Songs of Tyrtaeus: a literal prose translation. *Bohn's Class. Lib.* Bell, 1853.

\*CALVERLEY (C. S.) The Idylls of Theocritus: trans. into English verse. (1868.) Repr. Bell, 1913. (N.Y., Harcourt.)

> "As a characteristic specimen of the consummate art of the poet, and of the taste and skill of the translator, I

would point out the passage where Simaltha describes to her handmaid Thestylis the first visit of the young athlete whom she has summoned to cure her love-sickness. . . . If this be put beside the Greek, it will be seen how little of the finish of the original is lost; and a like comparison with the admirable prose version of Andrew Lang will show how faithful is the translation. One craves a verse-rendering of a poem like this. Lang's prose is perfectly graceful and full of poetry, but the metrical garb greatly enhances the charm. . . . Calverley has wonderfully maintained the charm of the Greek."—*R. Y. Tyrrell in the preface to Bell's reprint.*

*CHAPMAN (M. J.) The Greek pastoral poets: Theocritus, Bion and Moschus. London, 1836.

A verse translation of Theocritus reprinted with Banks's prose version entered above. "This version possesses very high merit, surpassing incomparably all predecessors, and not greatly, if at all, excelled by any successor."—*R. Kerlin in Theocritus in English Literature.*

EDMONDS (J. M.) Theocritus, Bion and Moschus: a prose translation. *Loeb Class. Lib.* Heinemann, 1912. (N.Y., Putnam.)

FAWKES (FRANCIS) The Idylliums of Theocritus and Bion. London. (1767.)

*HALLARD (J. H.) The Greek Bucolic Poets trans. into English verse. Longmans, 1894. Repr., revised, Routledge, 1920. *Broadway Translations Series.* (N.Y., Dutton.)

"The verse, where it can be compared with Dr. Way's, runs more smoothly and is less artificial. The translation has succeeded in being literal without being strained, and simple without being prosaic."—*A. S. Owen in Class. Rev.*, Vol. 30. *p.* 238.

"A version of great merit. It is scholarly, it follows the text closely. The 'Academy' (March 2, 1901) took 'it to be the best metrical version of Theocritus there is . . . it has the prime merit in a verse translation that it reads like good English verse!' "—*R. Kerlin in Theocritus in English Literature.*

HUNT (LEIGH) Five idylls and some passages. (1818.) Repr. O.U.P., 1924.

> These were published in the "Examiner" and in the "Jar of Honey". They will be found in the Oxford edition of Leigh Hunt's poetical works.

\*\*LANG (ANDREW) Theocritus, Bion and Moschus rendered into English prose. Macmillan. (1889.) Repr. *Golden Treasury Series*, 1924. (N.Y., Macmillan.)

> This has become almost an English classic itself. "Of Pindar and Theocritus we now possess prose versions as perfect, I believe, as any prose version of a poet can be. Mr. E. Myers's recent translation of Pindar and Mr. Lang's translation of Theocritus, Bion and Moschus preserve for us something even of the touch of the original. I am wont to look on Mr. Lang's Theocritus in particular, as a *tour de force* in translation at present without a rival. He has caught, although using prose, the music and lilt of the Greek verse."—*Frederic Harrison in The Choice of Books.*

MILLER (M. M.) and D. M. ROBINSON. Greek idylls; pastorals, songs, mimes, tales, epigrams: translated into rhymed verse. Lexington, Kentucky, Maxwelton Co., 1926.

SHELLEY (P. BYSSHE) Idylls. Repr. in O.U.P. edition, and other editions of his verse.

> Shelley made only three translations from Moschus and one from Bion, but they are beautifully done.

SYMONDS (J. A.) Idylls of Theocritus. In "Studies in the Greek Poets". (A. & C. Black, 1920.)

> Many scholars think that these fugitive translations represent the highest success yet attained in a verse rendering of the poems; they do not appear to have been published separately, but they appear as noted above, and also in many anthologies.

WAY (A. S) Theocritus, Bion and Moschus: a verse translation. C.U.P., 1913.

> "Despite the difficulty of rhyme and rhythm, Dr. Way succeeds in being singularly faithful for a verse translator."—*Class. Rev., Vol.* 27, *p.* 97.

> SUMMARY.—Amongst the bewildering number of translations of the Bucolic Poets, Lang's prose version and Calverley's and Hallard's poetical versions stand out as being the most successful and the most accessible versions of the whole works. Among the translators of odd poems here and there, Symonds takes a very high place.

# THEODORET
## (386–457)

ANONYMOUS. History of the Church, A.D. 322–427. *Bohn's Eccles. Lib.* Bell, 1854.

*See also* Apostolic Fathers (Appendix).

# THEOGNIS

## (Fl. 550 B.C.)

BANKS (J.) Elegies: a literal translation, with the metrical version of J. H. Frere. *Bohn's Class. Lib.* Bell. (N.Y., Macmillan.)

> Included in the volume which contains the works of Callimachus and Hesiod.

# THEOPHILUS

## (Fl. A.D. 170)

*See* Apostolic Fathers (Appendix).

# THEOPHRASTUS

## (d. 278 B.C.)

### *The Characters*

BUDGELL (EUSTACE) The Characters. London, 1713.

> "It was with me, as I believe it will be with all who look into this Translation; when I had begun to peruse it, I could not lay it by till I had gone through the whole Book. . . As for the translation, I have never seen any of a Prose Author which has pleased me more."—*Steele or Addison in "The Lover", No.* 39.

CLARK (R. T.) The Characters, together with the Mimes of Herodas, and the Tablet of Kebes. *New Univ. Lib.* Routledge, 1909. (N.Y., Dutton.)

EDMONDS (J. M.) The Characters. *Loeb Class. Lib.* Heinemann, 1929. (N.Y., Putnam.)

*HEALEY (J.) The Characters. *Temple Classics.* Dent, 1899. (N.Y., Dutton.)

Bound with Earle's "Microcosmographie".

**JEBB (SIR R. C.) Characters; with intro. and notes. Edited by Sir J. E. Sandys. Macmillan, 1909. (N.Y., Macmillan.)

### Other Works

HILL (SIR JOHN) History of stones: the Greek text, with an English version and notes. London, 1774.

HORT (SIR A. F.) Enquiry into plants and minor works on odours and weather signs. 2 vols. *Loeb Class. Lib.* Heinemann, 1916. (N.Y., Putnam.)

This is the first translation into English of the first-known book on botany. "Not only throws much light on the Greek, but also is very readable as original prose."— *Class. Rev., Vol.* 38, *p.* 38.

ROSS (W. D.) and F. H. Fobes. Metaphysics; with a trans. and a comm. O.U.P., 1930.

# THUCYDIDES

### (b. 471 B.C.)

*CRAWLEY (RICHARD) History of the Peloponnesian War. (1874.) Repr. in the *Temple Classics.* Dent, 1910. (N.Y., Dutton; Macmillan, 1874.)

HOBBES (THOMAS) History of the Grecian War. (1628.) Repr. edited by Sir W. Molesworth and W. B. Whittaker, 1845.

> The "Funeral Oration" was reprinted by the O.U.P. in 1929.
> An unequal piece of work, but with very considerable merits. "Bating his inaccuracy of detail (his Greek was not perfect, and the text was still in bad case) it is a masterpiece. Read him in the famous speeches . . . and Jowett seems a nerveless paraphrase."—*J. S. Phillimore in a pamphlet, Some remarks on translations and translators.*

**JOWETT (BENJAMIN) History of the Peloponnesian War. 2 vols. O.U.P., 1881.

> "All these three great works [i.e. Jowett's translations of Plato, Aristotle and Thucydides] are justly recognized as masterpieces of English."—*Sir J. Sandys, Hist. of Class. Scholarship, Vol. 3, p. 419.*

MARCHANT (E. C.) History of the Peloponnesian War. Bell, 1900.

> "In matters of criticism and interpretation, Marchant is ahead of Jowett and Dale."—*Class. Rev., Vol. 14, p. 183.*

SMITH (C. F.) History of the Peloponnesian War. 4 vols. *Loeb Class. Lib.* Heinemann, 1919. (N.Y., Putnam.)

ZIMMERN (ALICE E.) The Ideal of citizenship (Memorabilia). Lee Warner, 1916.


# TIMOCREON

(Fl. 479 B.C.)

Poetic fragments. *See* "Lyra Graeca" (Appendix).

# TRISMEGISTUS

*See* Hermes.

# TRYPHIODORUS

(Fl. A.D. 450)

*MAIR (A. W.) The Taking of Ilios: a prose translation.
*Loeb Class. Lib.* Heinemann, 1928. (N.Y., Putnam.)

> Included in a volume containing translations of Oppian
> and Coluthus.

MERRICK (JAMES) The Destruction of Troy: being the
sequel to the Iliad. Oxford, 1739.

# TYNNICHUS

(Date uncertain)

Poetic fragments. *See* "Lyra Graeca" (Appendix).

# TYRTAEUS

(Fl. 7th cent. B.C.)

BANKS (J.) War songs: a literal prose translation, with
the metrical version of R. Polwhele. *Bohn's Class.
Lib.* Bell, 1864.

> These translations are bound in the volume which also
> includes Theocritus, Bion and Moschus. Polwhele's
> version is considered an excellent translation. See also in
> Symond's *Greek Poets*.

# XANTHUS

(Fl. 650 B.C.)

Poetic Fragments. *See* "Lyra Graeca" (Appendix).

# XENOPHON

## (434–354 B.C.)

**\*DAKYNS (H. G.) Works. 4 vols. Macmillan, 1890–1897. (N.Y., Macmillan.)**

> There is a reprint of the Cyropaedia in the *Everyman's Library*. "Dakyns possessed a rare mastery of English idiom, as he was unusually well equipped for the work of a translator. His version will, I think, be found to satisfy those requirements of an effective translation which Professor Jowett laid down. It is faithful to the tone and the spirit of the original, and it has the literary quality of a good piece of original English writing."—*J. Hereford in the preface to the Everyman's reprint.*

**\*HOLLAND (PHILEMON) The Cyropaedia. London, 1632.**

**\*\*LOEB CLASSICAL LIBRARY. Xenophon's works. Heinemann, 1914–1920. (N.Y., Putnam.)**

> *Contents :*—Cyropaedia, by Walter Miller, 2 vols.; Hellenica, Anabasis, Symposium by C. L. Brownson and O. J. Todd, 3 vols; Scripta Minora, and Memorabilia and Oeconomicus by E. C. Marchant, 2 vols.
>
> Of Miller's translation: "A really satisfying translation which reproduces in admirable English the limpid simplicity of the original."—*J. M. Edmonds, Year's Work in Class. Studies,* 1912.
>
> Of Brownson's: "Mr. Brownson has completed his Anabasis in a plain, workmanlike style, well suited to its purpose. Mr. Todd is less successful with the Symposium; in dialogue especially his English is cumbrous. Mr. Marchant is as idiomatic in vocabulary and structure of sentences as Dakyns, but more simple and terse. . . . He has made an admirable book."—*H. Rackham, Class. Rev., Vol.* 38, *p.* 133.

MORGAN (M. H.) Xenophon on Horsemanship. Dent, 1894. (Boston, Little, Brown.)

SPELMAN (EDWARD) The Anabasis and Cyrus. London, 1742.

> This translation was highly praised by Gibbon, who thought it one of the most accurate and elegant prose translations that any language had produced.
>
> *See also* "Old Oligarch".

# XENOPHON OF EPHESUS

(Fl. 3rd cent. A.D.)

BEACH (W. W.) Abradates and Panthea. Salisbury, 1765.

ROOKE (?) The Love adventures of Abrocomas and Anthia. London, 1727.

> "A very good translation."—*Lowndes's Bibliographer's Manual.*
> This little tale is retold quite pleasantly in "Mr. Rooke's" version which reads with true eighteenth-century elegance.

# ZALEUCUS

(Fl. 650 B.C.)

TAYLOR (THOMAS) Political fragments. London, 1822.

> Included in the volume which contains the political fragments of Archytas and others.

# COLLECTIONS OF MINOR GREEK AUTHORS

## GREEK ANTHOLOGY

BURGES (G.) The Greek anthology: a literal translation into prose, with metrical versions by Bland, Merivale, etc. *Bohn's Class. Lib.* Bell, 1848. (N.Y., Macmillan.)

BUTLER (A. JOSHUA) Amaranth and Asphodel: versions of the Greek Anthology; Greek text and translation. Blackwell, 1922.

GARNETT (RICHARD) Selections from the Greek Anthology: translations by Richard Garnett, Andrew Lang, Goldwin Smith, and J. A. Symonds. *Canterbury Poets Series.* Walter Scott, 1889.

**GRUNDY (G. B.), Editor. Ancient gems in modern settings: being versions of the Greek Anthology in English rhyme by various writers. Blackwell, 1913.

> By far the best anthology of English versions of *the* Anthology. Some of the translations are by the editor, while others are his choice amongst the versions of Francis Fawkes (1721–1777) and other poets up to William Cory (1823–1892) whose exquisite "Heraclitus" is included.

LANG (ANDREW) The Grass of Parnassus: rhymes old and new. 1888.

> A selection of Lang's translations are included in the *Canterbury Poets Series* noted above.

*LEAF (WALTER) Little poems from the Greek. Two series. Grant Richards, 1925.

> "Dr. Leaf's versions are notable, achieving brevity and grace, a rare combination in English."—*V. Rendall in The London Mercury, Vol. II, p.* 333.

**MACKAIL (J. W.) Select epigrams from the Greek Anthology: text and translation. Longmans, 1891. Revised 1906.

> These exquisite little poems have achieved a lasting fame. From all points of view they are indispensable to the general reader and student alike.

**PATON (W. R.) The Greek Anthology: a prose translation, 5 vols. *Loeb Class. Lib.* Heinemann, 1920. (N.Y., Putnam.)

> "Admirable throughout, expressed in easy and natural English."—*Class. Rev., Vol.* 31, *p.* 142.
> The work has been done "with sympathy and skill. If the present writer confesses to finding a few blemishes . . . this is not to deny that the book as a whole is worthy to rank with Professor Mackail's 'Selections', and that means that its most important part, the translation, is about as good and true as a prose rendering of such little poems can be."—*J. M. Edmonds in The Year's Work in Class. Studies,* 1916.

TOMSON (GRAHAM R.) Selections from the Greek Anthology. Walter Scott.

WRIGHT (F. A.) The Girdle of Aphrodite: the complete love poems of the Palatine Anthology. *Broadway Translations*. Routledge, 1923.

> The poems in this book comprise the whole of the fifth book of the Palatine Anthology. The translations are not uniformly good, some of them being couched in language which is incongruously modern. In many, however, the author catches the spirit of the original in an engaging manner.

—— The Poets of the Greek Anthology: a companion volume to the "Girdle of Aphrodite". *Broadway Translations*. Routledge, 1924. (N.Y., Dutton.)

> *See also* Meleager.

# GREEK BUCOLIC POETS

# (i.e. THEOCRITUS, BION AND MOSCHUS)

*See* Theocritus.

# MISCELLANEOUS COLLECTIONS

EDMONDS (J. M.) Lyra Graeca. 3 vols. *Loeb Class. Lib.* Heinemann, 1922–27. (N.Y., Putnam.)

> Prose translations of all the Greek lyric poets from Eumelus to Timotheus except Pindar.

> *Contents :*—Alcaeus; Alcman; Anacreon; Apollodorus; Arion; Bacchylides; Corinna; Echembrotus; Ibycus; Lamprocles; Olympia; Polymnastus; Sacadas; Sappho; Simonides; Stesichorus; Telesilla; Terpander; Thelatas; Timocreon; Tynnichus; Xanthus, etc.

FELTON (C.) Ancient and modern Greece. 2 vols. Boston, Houghton, 1889.

> A standard work containing many fine original and quoted translations of lyrical and dramatic fragments. The version of the *Batrachomyomachia* is particularly noteworthy.

GARNETT (LUCY M. J.) Greek folk poesy: annotated translations from the whole cycle of Romaic folk-verse and folk-prose. Edited, with essays on the science of folk-lore, Greek folk-speech and the survival of paganism, by J. S. Stuart-Glennie. 2 vols. D. Nutt, 1896.

HEADLAM (WALTER) A Book of Greek verse. C.U.P., 1907. (N.Y., Macmillan.)

> Contains noteworthy translations of Greek lyrics.

HOWE (GEORGE) and G. A. HARRER. The Spirit of the classics. 2 vols. Vol. 1: Greek literature in translation. (N.Y., Harper, 1927.)

> An invaluable survey for the general reader. The notes and details, both literary and historical, are admirable. Translations are given of selections from the greatest writers, and from many minor authors. The latter include Callinus, Tyrtaeus, Archilochus, Alcaeus, Solon, Ibycus, Simonides, Mimnermus, Callistratus, Hybrias, etc.

MILLER (E. M.) and D. M. ROBINSON. Greek idylls; pastorals, songs, mimes, tales, epigrams: translated into rhymed verse. Lexington, Kentucky, Maxwelton Co., 1926.

> Mainly from Theocritus, Bion and Moschus.

POLLARD (A. W.) Editor. Odes from the Greek dramatists, trans. into lyric metres by English poets and
scholars. D. Stott, 1890.

SEDGWICK (J. M.) Love songs from the Greeks. Lane,
1896. (N.Y., G. H. Richmond.)

SHIPLEY (F. W.) Res gestae divi Augustae. *Loeb Class.
Lib.* Heinemann, 1924. (N.Y., Putnam.)

> Bound with the works of Velleius Paterculus. Another
> translation of the "Acts of Augustus" will be found in
> E. S. Shuckburgh's "Augustus", pages 293 to 301. (F.
> Unwin, 1908.)

STEBBING (WILLIAM) Greek and Latin anthology
thought into English verse. 3 vols. Unwin, 1923.

SYMONDS (J. A.) Studies of the Greek poets. Black,
1920.

> An indispensable book, from which an invaluable antho-
> logy could be made of some of the most successful trans-
> lations extant of Greek lyrics, including those of Sappho,
> Theocritus, and Herondas.

# PART THREE
# TRANSLATIONS FROM THE LATIN

# ABELARD AND HELOÏSE
## (1079-1142)

ANONYMOUS. Letters. Edited by H. Morten. Repr. from Watt's edition of 1722. *Temple Classics*. Dent, 1901. (N.Y., Dutton.)

> The only edition available for the ordinary reader. Some of the letters are foolishly bowdlerized.

*SCOTT-MONCRIEFF (C. K.) Letters. Trans. for the first time from the Latin. Guy Chapman, 1925. (N.Y., Knopf.)

> A beautiful translation, worthily produced. Its price, however, will place it beyond the reach of most readers.

# ACTS OF AUGUSTUS

*See* "Res Gestae Divi Augustae" (Greek Section—Appendix).

# ADAMNAN, SAINT
## (625–704)

FOWLER (J. T.) Prophecies, miracles and visions of St. Columba. O.U.P., 1895.

*HUYSHE (WENTWORTH) Life of St. Columba. *New Univ. Lib.* Routledge, 1906. (N.Y., Dutton.)

> By common consent, the best translation.

MACPHERSON (J. R.) The Pilgrimage of Arculfus in the Holy Land about the year A.D. 670. *Palestine Pilgrims' Text Society.* 1889.

# ADDISON, JOSEPH
## (1672–1719)

BOHN'S LIBRARY. Addison's Latin poems and prose.

> The complete Latin works of this author, together with translations by various hands, are included in Vol. 6 of the standard edition published by Bell, 1913. (N.Y., Macmillan.)

# AELIUS LAMPRIDIUS

*See* Lampridius.

# AENEAS SYLVIUS

*See* Pius II, *Pope.*

# AETNA, THE

ELLIS (ROBINSON) Aetna: a critical recension of the text, . . . with a prose translation, comm., and index. O.U.P., 1901.

> This famous poem is thought to be by Lucilius Junior. An earlier and much less scholarly version in verse will be found in Hughes' "Claudian", etc. London, 1741.

# AGRICOLA, GEORGIUS
## (1494–1555)

HOOVER (H. C. and L. H.) De re metallica. Trans. from the Latin edn. of 1556. *The Mining Magazine.* London, 1912.

# AILRED, SAINT

(St. Ailred of Rievaux, also known as Ethelred or Ealred)

(1109–1166)

FORBES (A. P.) The Life of St. Ninian. *Historians of Scotland Series*. Vol. 5. Edmonston and Douglas. Edinburgh, 1874.

# ÀKEMPIS, THOMAS

(1379–1471)

*ANONYMOUS. The Imitation of Christ. (1440.) *Everyman's Library*. Dent, 1910. (N.Y., Dutton.)

This edition is a recast of the earliest English translation.

BENHAM (W.) The Imitation of Christ. (1874.) Repr. in the *New Univ. Lib.* Routledge, 1905. (N.Y., Dutton.)

BIGG (C.) The Imitation of Christ. Methuen, 1905.

BYRNE (*Monsignor*) Vera sapientia; or, True wisdom. Burns and Oates, 1904. (N.Y., Benziger.)

*WHYTFORD (RICHARD) The Imitation of Christ. (1556.) Repr. Chatto and Windus, 1908; and in *The Orchard Books*, Burns and Oates. (N.Y., Benziger.)

"In style and feeling the finest rendering into English." —*D.N.B.*

# ALBINOVANUS, PEDO

### (Fl. 20 B.C.)

PLUMTRE (J.) The Elegies, with an English version. Kidderminster, 1807.

# ALCUIN

### (735–804)

GRIEVE (ALEXANDER) The Life of Willibrord, missionary in the Netherlands 691–739, including a trans. of the Vita Willibrordi of Alcuin. *Lives of Early and Medieval Missionaries.* S.P.C.K., 1923.

SLEE (J. M.) Letters. London, 1837.

# AMBROSE, SAINT

### (Fl. A.D. 397)

MANNIX (SISTER MARY DOLOROSA) Sancti Ambrosii Oratio obitu Theodosii: text, trans., intro., and comm. Catholic Univ. of Amer., Washington, 1925.

THOMPSON (T.) and J. H. SRAWLEY. On the Mysteries; and, The Treatise on the Sacraments by an unknown author. *Trans. of Christian Lit. Series.* S.P.C.K., 1919. (N.Y., Macmillan.)

*See also* Apostolic Fathers (Appendix).

[ 176 ]

# AMMIANUS MARCELLINUS

## (Fl. A.D. 360)

GIBBON (EDWARD) The Character of the Roman nobles.

> This translation will be found in Chapter 31 of "The Decline and Fall of the Roman Empire". Gibbon says: "It is incumbent on me to explain the liberties which I have taken with the text of Ammianus. (1) I have melted down into one piece the sixth chapter of the fourteenth and the fourth of the twenty-eighth book. (2) I have given order and connection to the confused mass of materials. (3) I have softened some extravagant hyperboles and pared away some superfluities of the original. (4) I have developed some observations which were insinuated rather than expressed". He then naïvely concludes: "With these allowances my version will be found, not literal indeed, but faithful and exact."—Note 34, Chapter 31.

HOLLAND (PHILEMON) Roman History. London, 1609.

YONGE (C. D.) Roman history. *Bohn's Class. Lib.* Bell, 1862. (N.Y., Macmillan.)

# ANDREWES, LANCELOT

## (Bishop of Ely, 1555–1626)

MEDD (P. G.) Private devotions. Christian Knowledge Society, 1899.

NEWMAN (J. H.) and J. M. NEALE. The Devotions. Repr. S.P.C.K., 1920. (N.Y., Macmillan.)

> The Greek portion was translated by Cardinal Newman and the Latin by Neale.

STANHOPE (DEAN) Private devotions. *Sanctuary Booklets.* Allenson, 1913. (Chicago, Blessing Co.)

# ANGLERIUS, PETER MARTYR

*See* Peter Martyr Anglerius.

# ANSELM, SAINT
## (1033–1109)

DEANE (S. N.) Proslogion, Monologion, and Cur Deus home. *Religion of Science Library*. K. Paul, 1903. (Chicago, Open Court Publ. Co.)

# ANTONINUS, AUGUSTUS

Itinerary through Britain. Trans. with additions in Camden's "Britannia", q.v.

# APOSTOLIC FATHERS

*See* Appendix.

# APULEIUS, L.
## (b. A.D. 114)

*ADLINGTON (WILLIAM) The Golden asse. (1566.) Repr. *Loeb Class. Lib.* Revised by S. Gaselee. Heinemann, 1915. (N.Y., Putnam.) *Abbey Classics*. Chapman and Dodd, 1922. (Boston, Small.) *Watergate Library*. Guy Chapman, 1923. (N.Y., Brentano.)

> "There exists only one English translation of 'The Golden asse' that repays reading. That is the translation of

Adlington, which for all its beauty, is inaccurate, and, what is more serious, exceedingly hard to procure."— *H. E. Butler*. (This was written in 1909. Since then three or more reprints have appeared.)

"As to the translation itself, much may be said both for and against. It is of course inaccurate . . . Adlington's scholarly equipment was not equal to the task of un-ravelling the author's dark and high style, with its fan-tastic caperings of word and phrase. . . . These faults, however, are slight. The English, young and vigorous, overcomes all weaknesses. It is simple, direct and fresh, and yet possesses that picturesque happiness of phrase which is the crown of a growing language. It is dignified, sonorous, but never heavy. . . . It is, indeed, as well rounded and as pleasant a piece of prose as you will meet in our tongue."—*Prof. Saintsbury in preface to the Abbey Classics reprint*.

Those who want Adlington's translation as he wrote it should procure the reprints in the *Abbey Classics* or *Watergate Series*.

BUTLER (H. E.) Apologia and Florida. O.U.P., 1909.

—— The Metamorphoses, or Golden Ass. 2 vols. O.U.P., 1910.

PATER (WALTER) Cupid and Psyche. (1892.)

A beautiful version of the episode of Cupid and Psyche in "The Golden ass" will be found in Vol. I, p. 66, of Pater's "Marius the Epicurean".

## AQUINAS, THOMAS

*See* Thomas, Saint.

# ARDERNE, JOHN
### (Fl. A.D. 1350)

POWER (SIR D'ARCY) De Arte phisicali et de cirugia.
Bale, Sons, and Danielsson, 1922. (N.Y., Wood.)

# ARETINO, LEONARDO

*See* Bruni, Leonardo.

# ARNOBIUS
### (Fl. A.D. 30)

*See* Apostolic Fathers (Appendix).

# ASSER, JOHANNES
### (Fl. A.D. 900)

COOK (A. S.) Life of King Alfred. (Boston, Ginn, 1906.)

GILES (J. A.) Life of King Alfred. In *Six Old English Chronicles. Bohn's Library.* Bell, 1848.

*JANE (L. C.) Life of King Alfred. *King's Library.* Chatto and Windus, 1908. (N.Y., Oxford Press.)

# AUGUSTINE, SAINT
### (354–430)
### *The City of God*

*DODS (MARCUS) City of God. In Schaff's *Library of Nicene and Post-Nicene Fathers, Vol.* 2. Clark. (N.Y., Scribner.)

HEALEY (JOHN) The City of God. (1610.) Repr. *Temple Classics*. 3 vols. Dent, 1903. (N.Y., Dutton.)

### The Confessions

*MATTHEW (SIR TOBIE) Confessions. (1620.) Repr. *Orchard Books*. Burns and Oates, 1923. (N.Y., Benziger.)

**PILKINGTON (J. G.) Confessions. Repr. in Schaff's *Library of Nicene and Post-Nicene Fathers, Vol.* 1. Clark. (N.Y., Scribner.)

PUSEY (E. B.) Confessions. (1838.) Repr. in *Scott Library*. Walter Scott, 1898. *Everyman's Library*. Dent, 1907. (N.Y., Dutton); Chatto and Windus, 1909.

WATTS (WILLIAM) Confessions. (1631.) Repr. in *Loeb Class. Lib.* 2 vols. Heinemann, 1925. (N.Y., Putnam.)

See also Apostolic Fathers (Appendix) for complete works.


## AUNGERVILLE, RICHARD
See Richard of Bury.


## AURELIUS ANTONINUS
See Greek Section.


## AUSONIUS, D. MAGNUS
(310–394)

BEAUMONT (SIR JOHN) Sixteen idylls in *Bosworth Field and other poems*. London, 1620.

*EVELYN-WHITE (H. G.) The Mosella: a prose transla-
tion. 2 vols. *Loeb Class. Lib.* Heinemann, 1921.
(N.Y., Putnam.)

> "Mr. White's version is easy and accurate."—*J. F. Dobson,
> The Year's Work in Class. Studies*, 1921–22.

*FLINT (F. S.) The Mosella: a verse translation. The
Egoist Press, 1915.

KENDALL (T.) Epigrams, in *Floures of epigrams*. London,
1577.

STANLEY (THOMAS) Ludus septem sapientum, in
*History of Philosophy*. London, 1743.

# AVIANUS, FLAVIUS

(Fl. 4th or 5th cent. A.D.)

L'ESTRANGE (SIR R.) Fables, in *Fables of Aesop, and
other eminent mythologists*. (1692.) Repr., 1879.

# BACON, FRANCIS

(1561–1626)

**ELLIS (R. L.) and J. SPEDDING. Works. 7 vols. (1857.)
Partly Repr. in 1 vol. Routledge, 1905. (N.Y.,
Longmans; Houghton.)

> The standard edition.

SHAW (P.) Advancement of learning. London, 1733.

*WOOD (H.) Novum organum. *Bohn's Library*. Bell, 1852. (N.Y., Macmillan.)

> A good version, highly esteemed by competent critics.

## BACON, ROGER

### (1214-1294)

BROWNE (RICHARD) Cure of old age, and preservation of youth. (1683.) Repr. in Sir J. Sinclair's *Code of Health*. 4 vols. Edinburgh, 1807.

BURKE (ROBERT BELLE) The Opus majus. 2 vols. University of Pennsylvania Press, 1928.

> Extraordinary as it may seem, this is the first translation into English of the most famous Latin treatise of the thirteenth century.

DAVIS (TENNEY L.) Letter concerning the marvellous power of art and of nature, and concerning the nullity of magic. Chemical Publ. Co., Easton, Pa., 1923. (English agents, Williams and Norgate.)

## BARCLAY, JOHN

### (1582-1621)

LE GRYS (SIR ROBERT) and THOMAS MAY. Argenis. London, 1629.

LONG (KINGSMILL) Argenis. London, 1625 and 1636.

MAY (THOMAS) The Mirrour of mindes. London, 1633.

REEVE (CLARA) The Phœnix; or, The History of Polyarchus and Argenis. 4 vols. London, 1772.

# BARTHOLOMEW

*See* Glanville, Bartholomew de.

# BEDE, THE VENERABLE

### (673-735)

SELLAR (A. M.) Ecclesiastical history. *Bohn's Lib.* Bell, 1917. (N.Y., Macmillan.)

WILCOCK. Lives of the Abbots of Wearmouth. Sunderland, 1818.

> *Note:* The most famous translation of Bede is, of course, King Alfred's Anglo-Saxon version.

# BENEDICT, SAINT

### (480-542)

GASQUET (F. AIDAN) The Rule of St. Benedict. Chatto and Windus, 1909.

MCCANN (DOM JUSTIN) The Rule, with the text, and a commentary by P. Delatte. Burns and Oates, 1921.

# BERNARD, SAINT (OF CLAIRVAUX)

## (1091–1153)

ANONYMOUS. Sermons and the treatise on consideration. Trans. by a Priest of Mount Melleray. 3 vols. Browne and Nolan, 1921.

EALES (S. J.) Some letters of St. Bernard, selected by F. A. Gasquet. Hodges, 1904. (St. Louis, Herder.)

GARDNER (E. G.) On the love of God: the Latin text and translation. Dent, 1916. (N.Y., Dutton.)

LAWLOR (H. J.) Life of St. Malachy of Armagh. *Trans. of Christian Lit. Series.* S.P.C.K., 1920. (N.Y., Macmillan.)

LEWIS (GEORGE) On consideration. O.U.P., 1908.

WILLIAMS (W. W.) On Grace and free will. *Trans. of Christian Lit. Series.* S.P.C.K., 1920. (N.Y., Macmillan.)

# BERNARD OF MORLAIX

## (Fl. A.D. 1140)

NEALE (J. M.) De contemptu mundi. Trans. as "The Rhythm of Bernard of Morlaix". Allenson, 1908.

PREBLE (HENRY) Source of Jerusalem the Golden, etc. (Univ. of Chicago Press.)

# BLACMAN, JOHN

### (Fl. A.D. 1440)

JAMES (M. R.) Life of Henry the 6th: a reprint, with trans. and notes. C.U.P., 1919.


# BLOSIUS, LUDOVICUS

### (François Louis de Blois. 1506–1566)

WILBERFORCE (BERTRAND A.) A Book of spiritual instruction, and comfort for the faint-hearted. 2 vols. Burns and Oates, 1925. (N.Y., Benziger.)


# BOCCACCIO, GIOVANNI

### (1313–1375)

GOLLANZ (SIR I.) Olympia: the Latin text of the fourteenth eclogue, trans. and edited. Chatto and Windus. *Medieval Library* and *At the Florence Press*, 1921.

LYDGATE (JOHN) De Casibus virorum et foeminarum illustrium (The Falle of princis, princessis and other nobles. (London, 1494.) Repr. Edit. by Dr. Henry Bergen. *E.E.T.S.* London, 1924.

> This work was "presented" by the Carnegie Institute of Washington. It forms the translation from the French prose of Lawrence de Premierfait's second and amplified version of Boccaccio's work.

# BOETHIUS, ANICIUS M.T.S.

## (470–525)

*ANONYMOUS. The Consolation of philosophy. Trans. by "I. T." (1609). Repr. edited by H. F. Stewart with the Tractates. *Loeb Class. Lib.* Heinemann. (N.Y., Putnam.)

> "The rendering is almost exact."—*H. F. Stewart.*

CHAUCER (GEOFFREY) The Consolation of philosophy. (1490.) Repr. O.U.P. and other editions.

**COLVILLE (GEORGE) The Consolation of philosophy. (1556.) Repr. *Tudor Library.* Nutt, 1897.

> "His work is one of the finest specimens we could desire of the rugged, terse, vigorous English of the sixteenth century. It is especially free from the euphuisms that characterize some of the Elizabethan writers."—*E. B. Bax in the intro. to the Tudor Library reprint.*

*COOPER (W. B.) The Consolation of philosophy. *Temple Classics.* Dent, 1902. (N.Y., Dutton.)

Fox (S.) King Alfred's Anglo-Saxon version of "The Consolation" with literal English translation on opposite pages. *Bohn's Lib.* Bell, 1848. (N.Y., Macmillan.)

SEDGEFIELD (W. J.) The Consolation of philosophy, done into modern English. O.U.P., 1900.

> SUMMARY.—Colville's translation is by far the best version of this pleasant work, but the reprint is now

almost as scarce as the original issue. Failing access to this, therefore, the translations in the *Temple Classics Series* and in the *Loeb Library* will be found both scholarly and readable.

## BONAVENTURA, SAINT
### (d. 1274)

COSTELLO (LAURENCE) Holiness of life (De perfectione vitae ad sorores). (St. Louis, Herder, 1923.)

DIVAS (DOMINIC) A Franciscan view of the spiritual and religious life: three treatises from the writings of St. Bonaventura. Baker, 1922. (N.Y., Benziger.)

LOVE (NICHOLAS) The Mirrour of the Blessed Lyf of Jesu Christ. (1410). Repr. ed. by L. F. Powell. Frowde, 1908. (N.Y., Benziger; Oxford Press.)

MOLLITOR (SABINUS) The Virtues of a religious superior (De sexalis seraphim). (St. Louis, Herder, 1920.)

SALTER (E. G.) Life of St. Francis. *Temple Classics.* Dent, 1904. (N.Y., Dutton.)

## BONIFACE, SAINT
### (d. A.D. 755)

KYLIE (EDWARD) The English correspondence of St. Boniface. *King's Classics.* Chatto and Windus, 1911. (N.Y., Oxford.)

# BOSCOVICH, RUGGIERO GIUSEPPE

(1711–1787)

CHILD (J. M.) A Theory of natural philosophy: a trans. with text. Open Court Publ. Co., 1922. (Chicago, Open Court Publ. Co.)

# BOURNE, VINCENT

(1695–1747)

COWPER (WILLIAM) The Latin poems of Vincent Bourne. (1800.) Repr. O.U.P. and other editions.

LAMB (CHARLES) Poems trans. from the Latin of Vincent Bourne.

> Seven poems will be found reprinted in Vol. 6 of Gibbings' edition of the collected works of Lamb, 1895, and in other collected editions.

# BRAVONIUS

*See* Florence of Worcester.

# BRUNI, LEONARDO

(Known as Aretino, 1369–1444)

GOLDYNG (ARTHUR) Historie of the Warres betweene the Imperialles and the Gothes for the possession of Italy. London, 1563.

# BRUTUS, JUNIUS

(Pseudonym.) *See* "Vindiciae contra tyrannos"


# BUCHANAN, GEORGE

(1506–1582)

BROWN (ARCHIBALD) Sacred dramas: trans. into English verse. Simpkin Marshall, 1906.

M'KECHNIE (W. S.) Verse translations of poems, etc., with notes. In "Glasgow Quatercentenary studies". Maclehose, 1907.

MILLAR (D. A.) George Buchanan: a memorial, 1506–1906. D. Nutt, 1907.
>    Contains translations of several of Buchanan's works.

MITCHELL (A. GORDON) Jepthes; and, John the Baptist. Gardner, 1902–1904.


# BURCHARD, JOHN

(Fl. 1500)

GLASER (F. L.) Pope Alexander VI and his court; extracts from the Latin diary. (N.Y., Brown, N. L., 1921.)

MATHEW (A. H.) The Diary of Johannes Burchardus, 1483–1506. Griffiths, 1910.
>    Only volume one of this work has been issued.

# BUSBECQ

(Ogier Ghiselin de Busbecq)

(1522–1592)

FORSTER (C. T.) and F. H. B. DANIELL. Life and letters. 2 vols. Kegan Paul, 1881.

FORSTER (E. S.) Turkish letters, newly translated from the Latin. O.U.P., 1927.

# BYNKERSHOEK, CORNELIUS VAN

(1673–1743)

DU PONCEAU (P. S.) A Treatise on the law of war. *American Law Journal, Vol.* 3. Philadelphia, 1808.

MAGOFFIN (RALPH VAN DEMAN) De Dominio maris dissertatio: a photographic reproduction . . . with an English translation. *Classics of International Law.* New York, 1923.

# CAELIUS FIRMIANUS SYMPOSIUS

*See* Symposius.

# CAESAR, C. JULIUS

(102–44 B.C.)

GOLDING (ARTHUR) Eight bookes of exploytes in Gallia and the countries bordering. London, 1565.

"Our earliest and best version."—*C. Whibley, Literary Studies, p.* 102.

*HOLMES (T. RICE) Gallic War. Macmillan, 1908. (N.Y., Macmillan.)

> This is recommended by scholars as a thoroughly adequate piece of work.

*LOEB CLASSICAL LIBRARY. Civil wars, by A. G. Peskett; Gallic War by H. J. Edwards. 2 vols. Heinemann, 1914, 1922. (N.Y., Putnam.)

LONG (F. P.) Gallic War. O.U.P., 1911.

—— Civil wars. O.U.P., 1906.

MACDEVITT (W. A.) Works of Caesar. Intro. by Thomas De Quincey. *Everyman's Library*. Dent, 1915 (N.Y., Dutton.)


# CAIUS, JOHN
### (1510–1573)

FLEMING (ABRAHAM) Of English dogges. London, 1576.

> This translation of "De canibus Britannicis" was reprinted in 1880 and again in 1912 in a volume of the works of John Caius, edited by E. S. Roberts.


# CALPURNIUS, T. JULIUS
### (Called Siculus. Fl. A.D. 50)

SCOTT (E. J. L.) Eclogues. Bell, 1891.

> "Mr. Scott is really something like a master of octosyllabic verse, into which he has translated the seven undoubted eclogues."—*Class. Rev., Vol.* 5, *p.* 327.

# CALVIN, JOHN

## (1509–1564)

CALVIN TRANSLATION SOCIETY. Works. 52 vols. Edinburgh, 1844–1856.

GOLDING (ARTHUR) Commentaries upon the prophet Daniell. London, 1570.

—— Sermons upon the Book of Job. London, 1574.

—— Treatise concerning offences. London, 1567.

WILES (J. P.) Instruction in Christianity: abbreviated edition of the Institutes of the Christian Religion. Dolby Bros. Stamford, 1921.

# CAMDEN, WILLIAM

## (1551–1623)

*GOUGH (R.) and J. NICHOLS. Britannia. 4 vols. London, 1806.

> This is the best edition.

HOLLAND (PHILEMON) Britannia. London, 1637.

NORTON (R.) Annals of the reign of Queen Elizabeth to 1588. London, 1630.

# CAPGRAVE, JOHN

## (1393–1464)

HINGESTON (F. C.) The Book of the illustrious Henries. 2 vols. London, 1858.

# CAPITOLINUS, JULIUS

(Fl. A.D. 300)

Lives. *See* "Scriptores Historiae Augustae" (Appendix).


# CASSIANUS, JOHANNES

(360–448)

*See* Apostolic Fathers (Appendix).


# CASSIODORUS, MAGNUS AURELIUS

(c. 480–575)

HODGKIN (T.) Letters: a condensed version of the *Variae Epistolae*. O.U.P., 1886.

> This translation was very highly thought of by the late Professor W. P. Ker.


# CATO, DIONYSIUS

(Date uncertain)

BURGH (BENEDICT) Parvus Cato; Magnus Cato: trans. into English verse, with the text. (1479.) Repr. C.U.P., 1906. (N.Y., Macmillan.)

> The reprint is edited by F. J. H. Jenkinson and is included in a series of photogravure facsimiles of rare fifteenth-century books, printed in England and now in the Univ. Lib. of Cambridge.

CHASE (WAYLAND J.) The Distichs of Cato. (Madison, Univ. of Wisconsin). Studies in the Social Sciences and History, No. 7. 1922.

FRANKLIN (Benjamin) Moral distichs: Englished in couplets. Philadelphia, 1735.

## CATO, M. PORCIUS
### (234–149 B.C.)

HARRISON (FAIRFAX) De re rustica: eclogues from Cato's Farm Management. Chicago, 1910.

—— Roman farm management. Macmillan, 1913. (N.Y., Macmillan.)

## CATULLUS, C. VALERIUS
### (84–54 B.C.)

ALLEN (G.) The Attis: trans. into English verse, with text and dissertations. D. Nutt, 1892.

BOHN'S CLASSICAL LIBRARY. Catullus, Tibullus and the Vigil of Venus: a literal prose translation with intro. and notes and the metrical versions of Lamb, Grainger, Thomas Moore, Elton, Nott, Otway, Hodgson, Leigh Hunt, Parnell, Thomas Stanley, etc. Bell, 1850. (N.Y., Macmillan.)

*CORNISH (F. W.) Catullus: a prose translation. *Loeb Class. Lib.* Heinemann, 1912. (N.Y., Putnam.)

The translation of "Tibullus" by J. P. Postgate and of the "Pervigilium Veneris" by J. W. Mackail is included in this volume. Of the "Catullus", Robinson Ellis writes: "The version is perhaps a little unequal: it has its tame or unworked passages, chiefly in the less interesting or more objectionable poems."—*Class. Rev., Vol.* 18.

This edition in the *Loeb Library* is a reprint of the 1904 edition, published by the C.U.P., and still obtainable.

**\*\*DUCKETT (ELEANOR SHIPLEY) Catullus in English poetry. *Smith Coll. Class. Studies.* (Northampton, Mass., 1925.)**

> An invaluable anthology of the finest renderings of Catullus drawn from various sources, ranging in authorship from John Skelton to Andrew Lang and contemporary poets. The Latin text is also given.

**ELLIS (ROBINSON) The Poems and fragments of Catullus: trans. in the metres of the original. Murray, 1871.**

**\*LAMB (GEORGE) The Poems of Caius Catullus. London, 1821.**

> Some of these are included in the *Bohn* selection entered above. They are very readable, but it has been objected that, owing to the influence of Pope, Lamb sacrificed the simplicity of Catullus for antithesis. "A very successful translation, especially good in the rendering of the lighter and more sportive poems."—*F. A. Wright in his edition of Catullus.*

**\*MACNAGHTEN (HUGH) The Poems of Catullus, done into English verse. (1899.) C.U.P., 1925.**

> Like most of the work of this scholar, these versions are delicate and effective. "Some of the versions are as good as can be."—*Class. Rev., Vol.* 41, *p.* 64.

MARRIS (SIR W.) Catullus, trans. into English verse, with text. O.U.P., 1924.

> "Scholarly, straightforward, forcible . . . the book will take a worthy place among verse translations."—*Class. Rev., Vol.* 40, *p.* 75.

MARTIN (SIR THEODORE) The Poems of Catullus: a verse translation. London, 1861.

QUILLER-COUCH (SIR A.) The Vigil of Venus and other poems. Methuen, 1912.

SYMONS (ARTHUR) From Catullus, chiefly concerning Lesbia: Latin and English texts. Secker, 1924.

SYMONS-JEUNE (J. F.) Some Poems of Catullus: a verse translation. Heinemann, 1923.

> "To appreciate a *tour de force* of this kind one must know Catullus well; . . . He [the translator] is best in the lighter pieces."—*J. Harrower, Class. Rev., Vol.* 38, *p.* 174.

TYTLER (H. W.) Coma Berenices: trans. into verse. *Bohn's Class. Lib.* Bell, 1876.

> "Coma Berenices" was originally written in Greek by Callimachus, but this work is not extant. Catullus translated it into Latin, and Tytler's version of this work will be found in the volume containing the works of Hesiod, Callimachus and Theognis.

*WRIGHT (F. A.) The Complete poems of Catullus. *Broadway Trans.* Routledge, 1926. (N.Y., Dutton.)

> Also includes a selection of the most successful translations by Sidney, Cowley, Crashaw, Campion, Ben

Jonson, Swift, Leigh Hunt, Byron, Landor, J. H. Frere, G. S. Davies and J. Wight Duff.

SUMMARY.—Translations of these poems are almost as numerous as those of Horace, and new attempts appear almost every year. The best prose translation is that in the *Loeb Classical Library*, and the selection in *Bohn's* series and that in the *Broadway Translations* are particularly recommended because they form in themselves a kind of anthology of the best versions. For American readers, and indeed for all who can obtain it, Miss E. S. Duckett's anthology is by far the best of its kind, although some of the poems she quotes as showing the influence of Catullus on modern writers are often neither good poems in themselves nor particularly noteworthy as classical echoes. Sir Richard Burton's translation (1894) attracted attention more by reason of the translator's eminence than by its merit.

# CELSUS, CORNELIUS

### (Fl. 20 B.C.)

GREIVE (JAMES) Of medicine: trans. with notes. London, 1756 and 1837.

UNDERWOOD (J. W.) Eight books on medicine literally translated. London, 1830.

# CENSORINUS

### (A.D. 238)

MAUDE (WILLIAM) De Die natale ("The Natal day"). Camb. Ency. Co., N.Y., 1900.

# CICERO, M. TULLIUS

(106–43 B.C.)

*Loeb Classical Library. Complete works. Heine-
mann, 1912. (N.Y., Putnam.) *In Progress.*

> De Finibus, De Natura Deorum, by H. Rackham; De
> Officiis, by Walter Miller; Letters to Atticus, by E. O.
> Winstedt; De Senectute, De Amicitia, De Divinatione, by
> W. A. Falconer; Speeches, by N. H. Watts; Ad Familiares
> Letters, by W. G. Williams; Catiline Orations, Pro Murena,
> Pro Flaeco, Pro Sulla, by R. L. Ullman; De Oratore, by
> C. Stuttaford; De Re Publica, De Legibus, by Clinton W.
> Keyes; The Verrine Orations, L. H. G. Greenwood.

### The Offices

Cockman (T. C.) The Offices. (1699.) Repr. *Everyman's
Library.* Dent, 1910. (N.Y., Dutton.)

> Included in this volume is Melmoth's translation of the
> "Letters."

*L'Estrange (Sir Roger) The Offices. (1720.) Repr.
*Temple Classics.* Dent, 1900. (N.Y., Dutton.)

> "He did his work of translation with the utmost thorough-
> ness. . . . His chiefest qualification for the task was his
> mastery of his own language."—*Charles Whibley, Camb.
> Hist. Eng. Lit., Vol. 9.*

### Letters

Melmoth (W.) Essays on friendship, old age; and,
Select letters. (1753–1777.) Repr. of Letters only
in *Everyman's Library.* Dent, 1910. (N.Y., Dutton.)

> A good piece of work.

*SHUCKBURGH (E. S.) The Whole extant correspond-
ence. 4 vols. Bell, 1899. (N.Y., Harcourt.)

> "On the whole, a high standard of excellence is main-
> tained. I have found the translation decidedly readable."
> —*W. W. Fowler, Class. Rev., Vol.* 14, *p.* 421.

### The Orations

GUTHRIE (W.) The Orations. (1741.) Repr. edited by
F. W. Norris. *Scott Library.* Scott, 1900. (N.Y.,
Simmons.)

## CLAUDIAN
### (Claudius Claudianus, d. A.D. 408)

DIGGES (LEONARD) The Rape of Proserpine. London,
1617.

HAWKINS (A.) Works: trans. into English verse, 2 vols.
London, 1817.

HUGHES. Two books against Rufinus: a verse translation. London, 1737.

> "Held in considerable estimation."—*Moss, Manual of
> Class. Bibliog.*

PLATNAUER (M.) Works: a prose translation. 2 vols. *Loeb
Class. Lib.* Heinemann, 1922. (N.Y., Putnam.)

## CLAVIUS, CHRISTOPHER
### (1537–1612)

ANDERSON (G.) Arenarius, trans. from the Greek of
Archimedes, to which is added the Dissertation
of Christopher Clavius on the same subject in
Latin. London, 1784.

# COLUMELLA, L. JUNIUS MODERATUS
### (Date uncertain)

CURTIUS (M. C.) Of husbandry (De re rustica) and his book concerning trees. London, 1745.

# COMENIUS, JOHN AMOS
### (Known as Komenski. 1592–1671)

KEATINGE (M. W.) The Great didactic, Englished for the first time. Black, 1896. (N.Y., Macmillan.)

LUTZOW (COUNT) Labyrinth of the world, and the Paradise of the Heart. *Temple Classics*. Dent, 1905. (N.Y., Dutton.)

MONROE (W. S.) The School of infancy. *Pedagogical Lib*. (Boston, D. C. Heath.) 1897.

# CURTIUS RUFUS, Q.
### (Fl. 1st cent. A.D.)

BRENDE (JOHN) Historie . . . contayning the actes of the Great Alexander, etc. London, 1602.

CODRINGTON (THOMAS) The Life and death of Alexander the Great. London, 1652.

DIGBY (JOHN) History of the wars of Alexander. (1714.) Rev. by W. M. Young. 2 vols. London, 1747.

KNIGHT (H. J. C.) Works: literally trans. with marginal headings and a life of Alexander the Great. Hall and Son, Cambridge, 1882.

MacCRINDLE (J. W.) History of Alexander the Great: Book VIII (Ch. 9–14) and Book IX of Quintus Curtius. Constable, 1893.

> The full title is "The Invasion of India by Alexander the Great, as described by Arrian, Quintus Curtius, etc. . . ."

THOMPSON (J.) Quintus Curtius: Book IX (Ch. 6 to the end). U.T.P., 1904.


# CYPRIAN, SAINT
### (d. A.D. 258)

BINDLEY (T. H.) On the Lord's Prayer. *Church Class. Series.* 1898.

BLAKENEY (E. H.) De unitate ecclesiae; trans. with intro. and brief notes. S.P.C.K., 1928 (N.Y., Macmillan.)

GEE (H.) On the Lord's Prayer. Bell, 1904.

LACEY (T. A.) Select epistles treating of the Episcopate, after the translation of Nathaniel Marshall. S.P.C.K., 1922. (N.Y., Macmillan.)

NEWMAN (J. H.) Treatises and Epistles. 2 vols. *Lib. of the Fathers.* J. H. and J. Parker, 1840–44.

WALLIS (R. E.) The Writings of St. Cyprian. 2 vols. *Ante-Nicene Fathers.* Clark, 1867. (N.Y., Scribner.)

# DANTE ALIGHIERI

## (1265-1321)

BREWER (WILMON) Eclogues (the poetical correspondence between Dante and Giovanni del Virgilio. Trans. into Eng. blank verse. (Boston, Cornhill Publ. Co.)

BROMLEY (C. H.) A Question of the water and the land: trans. with intro. and notes. Nutt, 1897.

HOWELL (A. G. FERRERS) Treatise: De Vulgari Eloquentia. (K. Paul, 1890.) Repr. *Temple Classics*. Dent, 1904. (N.Y., Dutton.)

SHADWELL (C. L.) A Question of the water and the land. O.U.P., 1909.

*TEMPLE CLASSICS. A Translation of the Latin works. 2 vols. Dent, 1904. (N.Y., Dutton.)

> *Contents :*—De Vulgari eloquentia, by A. G. F. Howell; De Monarchia, Epistolae, Eclogae and Quaestio de aqua et terra, by P. H. Wicksteed.

*TOYNBEE (PAGET) Letters: amended text, intro., notes and trans. O.U.P., 1920.

WHITE (A. CAMPBELL) Quaestio de aqua et terra: a trans. and a discussion of its authenticity. (Harvard Univ. Pr.)

WICKSTEED (P. H.) De Monarchia, Epistolae, Eclogae and Quaestio de aqua et terra. *Temple Classics*. Dent, 1904. (N.Y., Dutton.)

## DESCARTES, RÉNÉ
### (1596–1650)

*HALDANE (E. S.) and G. R. T. ROSS. Philosophical works: rendered into English. 2 vols. C.U.P., 1912. (N.Y., Macmillan.)

SMITH (D. E.) and M. L. LATHAM. Geometry, trans. from the Latin and French. (Chicago, Open Court Publ. Co.)

VEITCH (JOHN) The Method, meditations and selections from the "Principles"; trans. from the original French and Latin, with a new intro., essay, historical and critical. (1850.) Repr. Blackwood, 1907. (Chicago, Open Court Publ. Co.)

## DONATUS, AELIUS
### (Fl. A.D. 360)

CHASE (W. J.) The Ars minor, trans. with introductory sketch. 55 pp. (Univ. of Wisconsin Studies, Madison, 1926.)

## DUFRESNOY, CHARLES ALPHONSE
### (1611–1665)

DRYDEN (JOHN) De Arte graphica (The Art of painting). Trans. into English prose together with an original preface. London, 1695.

*MASON (W.) The Art of Painting. Trans. into Engl. verse, with annotations. Latin text included. York, 1783. Repr. in Mason's complete works, Vol. 3, 1811.

# DUPLESSIS MORNAY

*Supposed author* of "Vindiciae contra tyrannos," *q.v.*

# DURANDUS, WILLIAM
## (1237–1296)

NEALE (J. M.) and B. WEBB. The Symbolism of churches: being Book I of the "Rationale Divinorum Officiorum". Leeds, 1843. (N.Y., Scribner.)

PASSMORE (T. H.) The Sacred vestments: an English rendering of the 3rd Book of the "Rationale Divinorum Officiorum". Low, 1899.

# EALRED
*See* Ailred.

# EBO AND HERBORDUS
## (Fl. 1150)

ROBINSON (C. H.) The Life of Otto, Apostle of Pomerania, 1060–1139. S.P.C.K., 1920. (N.Y., Macmillan, 1921.)

# EDDIUS STEPHANUS
### (Fl. A.D. 669)

COLGRAVE (B.) Life of Bishop Wilfrid of York: text, trans., notes, etc. C.U.P., 1927. (N.Y., Macmillan.)


# EGINHARD
### (770–820)

GLAISTER (W.) Life of Emperor Karl the Great. London, 1877.

GRANT (A. J.) The Life of Charles the Great (Charlemagne). In "Early lives of Charlemagne". *Mediaeval Library*. Chatto and Windus, 1922. (N.Y., Oxford Press.)

> Contains also the life by the "Monk of St. Gall."

PREBLE (HENRY) Letters. (N.Y., 1913.)

WENDELL (BARRETT) History of the translation of the Blessed Martyrs of Christ. (Harvard Univ. Press, 1926.)


# ENNIUS
### (239–169 B.C.)
*See* Howe and Harrer (Appendix).


# "EPISTOLAE OBSCURORUM VIRORUM"
*See* Gratius, Ortwinus.

# ERASMUS, DESIDERIUS
## (1466–1536)

### Complaint of peace
GRIEVE (ALEXANDER), *Editor*. Complaint of peace, trans. 1559. Repr. Headley, 1917.

### The Colloquies
**BAILEY (N.) Familiar colloquies. (1725.) Repr. Gibbings. 1905. (N.Y., Scribner.)

*L'ESTRANGE (SIR ROGER) Twenty select colloquies. (1680.) Repr., intro. by C. Whibley. *Abbey Classics*. Chapman and Dodd, 1923. (Boston, Small.)

> "He did his work of translation with the utmost thoroughness. . . . His chiefest qualification for the task was his mastery of his own language. [In his Erasmus] the translator produces the impression of a living book—not the best of living books, truly, for there is sometimes a flippancy of phrase in L'Estrange's version."—*C. Whibley, Camb. Hist. Eng. Lit.*, *Vol.* 9.

### In praise of folly
*CHALONER (SIR THOMAS) In praise of folly. (1569.) Repr., ed. by J. E. Ashbee. Arnold, 1901.

WILSON (JOHN) In praise of folly. (1668.) Repr., ed. by P. S. Allen. O.U.P., 1913.

### The Letters
FROUDE (J. A.) Life and letters of Erasmus. Longmans, 1894.

> "An excellent translation of Erasmus' letters, which admirably reflects the terseness, the vivacity and the wit of the original; interspersed with references, and remarks by Froude to enable the reader to keep hold of the main thread."—*Athenæum*.

*NICHOLLS (F. M.) Epistles: from his earliest letters to his fifty-first year. 3 vols. Longmans, 1901–1918. (N.Y., Longmans.)

## ETHELRED

*See* Ailred.

## ETHELWERD, FABIUS
### (d. *c*. A.D. 998)

GILES (J. A.) Chronicle, to A.D. 975. In "Six Old English Chronicles". *Bohn's Lib*. Bell, 1848.

## ETNA

*See* Aetna.

## EUTROPIUS
### (d. A.D. 370)

CLARKE (JOHN) Epitome of the Roman history. York, 1722.

THOMAS. Epitome of the Roman history. London, 1760.

> "A good one, less literal than Clarke's, more accurate."—*Lowndes's Bibliographer's Manual*.

WATSON (J. S.) Epitome of the Roman history. *Bohn's Class. Lib*. Bell, 1882.

> A literal translation bound with the works of Justin and Cornelius Nepos.

# FASTIDIUS

(5th cent. A.D.)

HASLEHURST (R. S. T.) Works, with a parallel text and translation. Soc. of SS. Peter and Paul, 1927.

# THE FATHERS, THE WRITINGS OF

*See* Apostolic Fathers (Appendix).

# FIRMIANUS SYMPOSIUS

*See* Symposius.

# FLACCUS, VALERIUS

(Fl. A.D. 50)

BLOMFIELD (H. G.) The Argonautica: a prose translation of Book I. Blackwell, 1916. (N.Y., Longmans.)

> "In the main the result obtained has been readable and forcible, though it seems . . . to have erred on the side of diffuseness and prolixity."—*J. Wight Duff, Class. Rev., Vol. 30, p. 234.*

# FLORENCE OF WORCESTER

(d. A.D. 1118)

FORESTER (T). Chronicle. *Bohn's Ant. Lib.* Bell, 1854.

STEVENSON (J.) Chronicle. *Church Historians of England,* 1853.

# FLORUS, L. ANNAEUS
## (Fl. A.D. 100)

CASAUBON (MERIC) Roman histories. London, 1659.

DAVIES (JOHN) Florus: trans. into English. London, 1667.

FORSTER (E. S.) Epitome of Roman history, with an English translation. *Loeb Class. Lib.* Heinemann. (N.Y., Putnam.)

WATSON (J. S.) Epitome of Roman history. *Bohn's Lib.* Bell, 1852.

> A literal translation bound with the works of Sallust and Velleius Paterculus.

# FORTESCUE, SIR JOHN
## (1394-1476)

GREGOR (FRANCES) De laudibus legum Angliae (Commendation of the laws of England). Sweet and Maxwell, 1917.

# FRONTINUS, S. JULIUS
## (Fl. A.D. 70)

BENNETT (C. E.) and C. HERSCHEL. Stratagems and aqueducts of Rome. *Loeb Class. Lib.* Heinemann, 1925. (N.Y., Putnam.)

HERSCHEL (CLEMENS). The Two books on the water supply of the city of Rome: a photographic reproduction of the sole original Latin MS., and its reprint in Latin; also a translation with explanatory chapters. Longmans, 1913. (Boston, Estes.)

# FRONTO, M. CORNELIUS
### (Fl. A.D. 140)

HAINES (C. R.) Correspondence. 2 vols. *Loeb Class. Lib.* Heinemann, 1919. (N.Y., Putnam.)

> The correspondence of Fronto with Marcus Aurelius has never before been translated into English.

# GAIUS
### (Fl. A.D. 150)

ABDY (J. T.) and B. WALKER. Commentaries: Latin text with trans. and notes. C.U.P., 1870. (N.Y., Macmillan.)

POSTE (E.) Institutionum juris civilis commentarii quatuor, with a trans. and a commentary. O.U.P.

Elements of Roman Law. O.U.P., 1890.

TRAPNELL (J. G.) The Institutes (Extracts) Title xlv. Macmillan, 1908.

# GALLICANUS VULCATIUS

*See* Vulcatius.

# GALLUS, C. CORNELIUS

(B.C. 66–26)

WALKER (HOVENDEN) The Impotent lover: accurately described in six elegies on old age, with the old doting letcher's resentment on the past pleasures and vigorous performances of youth: a verse translation. London, 1689.

# GELLIUS, AULUS

(Fl. A.D. 150)

BELOE (WILLIAM) Attic nights. London, 1795.

> "Contains numerous errors and omits many words and phrases."—*J. C. Rolfe.*

*ROLFE (J. C.) Attic nights. 3 vols. *Loeb Class. Lib.* Heinemann, 1927. (N.Y., Putnam.)

# GENNADIUS

*See* Apostolic Fathers (Appendix).

# GEOFFREY OF MONMOUTH
### (1100–1154)

EVANS (SEBASTIAN) Historia regum Britanniae. *Temple Classics* and *Everyman's Library*. Dent, 1903. (N.Y., Dutton.)

GILES (J. A.) Historia regum Britanniae. In "Six Old English chronicles". *Bohn's Lib*. Bell, 1848.


# GESTA ROMANORUM
### *See* Appendix.


# GETA, HOSIDIUS
### (Fl. A.D. 170)

MOONEY (J. J.) Hosidius Geta's tragedy "Medea", a Virgilian cento, Latin text with metrical trans., with an outline of ancient Roman magic. Birmingham, Cornish Bros., 1919.


# GHISELIN DE BUSBECQ
### *See* Busbecq.


# GILBERT, WILLIAM
### (1540–1603)

GILBERT CLUB. On the magnet, magnetick bodies, also, etc. London, 1900.

Mottelay (P. F.) On the lodestone and magnetic bodies and on the great magnet, the earth. Quaritch, 1893. (N.Y., Wiley.)

# GILDAS
### (*c.* 500–570)

Giles (J. A.) Historical works. In "Six Old English chronicles". *Bohn's Lib.* Bell, 1848.

# GIRALDUS DE BARRI,
## *called* CAMBRENSIS
### (1146–1220)

Bohn's Antiquarian Library. The Works of Giraldus Cambrensis. Bell, 1863.

> *Contents :*—History of the conquest of Ireland, by T. Forester; and, Itinerary through Wales, by R. C. Hoare. Revised by T. Wright.

Williams (W. L.) The Itinerary and description of Wales. *Everyman's Library.* Dent, 1908. (N.Y., Dutton.)

# GLANVILLE, BARTHOLOMEW DE
### (Bartholomaeus Anglicus)
### (Fl. A.D. 1230)

Trevisa (John de) De Proprietatibus rerum. (1398.) Repr. under the title of "Mediaeval lore", edited by Robert Steele, 1893; and in the *Mediaeval Library*, Chatto and Windus, 1924.

# GRATIUS FALISCUS

## (40 B.C.–A.D. 20)

WASE (CHRISTOPHER) Cynegeticon; or, A Poem of hunting with dogs. London, 1654.


# GRATIUS, ORTWINUS

## (1448–1542)

STOKES (F. G.) Epistolae obscurorum virorum: Latin text with English rendering, notes, etc. Chatto and Windus, 1909. (N.Y., Oxford Press.)

> A vigorous rendering of these famous letters, addressed satirically to the Dutch philosopher, Ortwin von Graes.


# GREGORY THE FIRST, SAINT

## (Surnamed the Great. 540–604)

BARMBY (JAMES) Works. *Nicene and Post-Nicene Fathers, Vol.* 12. Clark, 1895. (N.Y., Scribner.)

MARRIOTT (CHARLES) Morals on the Book of Job. 3 vols. *Lib. of the Fathers.* J. H. and J. Parker, 1844–50.

P. W. Dialogues. (1608.) Repr., ed. by E. G. Gardner. Medici Soc., 1911.

*See also* Apostolic Fathers (Appendix).

[ 215 ]

# GREGORY OF TOURS
(540–594)

DALTON (O. M.) History of the Franks. 2 vols. O.U.P., 1927.

> "His book has two parts. The second volume is an accurate and workmanlike translation of the text (not at all an easy thing to make), with a large number of explanatory and illustrative notes, textual as well as historical, which are extraordinarily complete, as well as clear and compact. We cannot praise this too highly. The first volume is of an introductory and general nature."—*Times Lit. Supp., July* 28, 1927.
>
> In 1917 the Columbia University Press (English agents, O.U.P.) issued a useful selection of the "History of the Franks", translated, with notes, by E. Brehaut.

# GROTIUS, HUGO
(Huig van Groot. 1583–1645)

*Miscellaneous Works*

BARHAM (A. F.) Adamus Exul; or, the Prototype of Paradise lost. London, 1847.

GOLDSMID (E.) On the origin of the native races of America. 1884.

MAGOFFIN (RALPH VAN DEMAN) The Freedom of the Seas. Trans. with revision of the Latin text of 1633. Ed. by J. B. Scott. *Carnegie Endow. for Intern. Peace.* 1916.

MANLEY (T.) De Rebus Belgicis. London, 1665.

SANDYS (GEORGE) Christ's Passion. (1640.) Repr. J. R. Smith, London, 1885.

SEDGER (T.) On the truth of the Christian religion: literal trans. with notes. London, 1859.

*The Rights of War and Peace*

CAMPBELL (A. C.) The Rights of war and peace. Pontefract, 1814.

*KNIGHT (W. S. N.) Selections from the "Rights of war and peace": trans. with intro. *Texts for Students of International Relations*. London, 1922.

WHEWELL (W.) Rights of war and peace: abridged trans. Cambridge, 1853. (N.Y., Putnam.)

# HARVEY, WILLIAM
## (1578-1657)

LEAKE (C. D.) Exercitatio anatomica de motii cordis et sanguinis in animalibus. Baillière, 1928.

WILLIS (R.) Works, with a life. Sydenham Soc., 1847.
> The most famous of Harvey's works—"The Circulation of the blood"—was reprinted from this edition, in *Everyman's Library*. Dent, 1907. (N.Y., Dutton.)

# HENRY OF HUNTINGDON
## (1084-1155)

FORESTER (T.) History of the English from the Roman Invasion to Henry II, with the Acts of King Stephen. *Bohn's Lib*. Bell, 1853.

# HERMES TRISMEGISTUS

*See* Greek Section.

# HIERONYMUS

*See* Jerome, Saint.

# HIGDEN, RALPH
### (d. 1364)

JOHN OF TREVISA. Polychronicon. (1387.) Text and trans. repr., ed. by C. Babington and J. R. Lumby. 9 vols. 1865–1886.

# HILARY, SAINT (OF POITIERS)
### (A.D. 300–366)

WATSON (E. W.) and others. Select works. *Lib. of Nicene and Post-Nicene Fathers.* 2nd series. Vol. 9. Clark, 1890. (N.Y., Scribner.)

# HORACE
### (Q. Horatius Flaccus. 65–8 B.C.)

BEAUMONT (SIR JOHN) Twenty-ninth ode of Book III. In "Bosworth Field". London, 1629. Repr. in the *Chandos Classics* and in Jourdain's collection in the *Temple Classics, q.v.*

> "A really beautiful piece of work. By far the finest among the translations of Horace" [before 1641].—*Victor Scholderer in Palmer's List of translations before* 1641.

BLAKENEY (E. H.) On the art of poetry: Latin text, English prose translation, intro. and notes; with Ben Jonson's English verse rendering. Scholartis Pr., 1928.

> A very good rendering, worthily produced. The introduction and notes are valuable and full of scholarly allusion. It is good, too, to have Ben Jonson's version placed again in print after many years of neglect.

**BUTLER (H. E.), *Editor*. The Odes: rendered in English verse by various hands, with the Latin text. Bell, 1929.

*CALVERLEY (C. S.) Odes. Bell, 1901.

> In the complete works of Calverley will be found the fifteen odes which he translated. They are taken from Books I, III and IV, and are thought to be among the best works of this gifted translator.

**CHANDOS CLASSICS. Works of Horace. Warne, 1889.

> This volume comprises an anthology of the most successful and famous translations of Horace from the sixteenth to the nineteenth century. The "Art of poetry" is by Francis, while the "Epistles" are either by Howes or by Francis. The minor poems include translations by the following authors: Dryden, Milton, Francis, Howes, Lytton, Evelyn, Pitt, Calverley, Congreve, Dr. Johnson, Conington, Fanshawe, Hartley Coleridge, Sedley, Cowper, Crashaw, Otway, Sir T. Martin, Cowley, Swift, Addison, Ben Jonson and Barry Cornwall.

**CONINGTON (J.) The Works of Horace. (1870.) Repr. Bell, 1905. (N.Y., Harcourt.)

> "So far as I can learn, it holds the field as the standard verse translation, and it is a good piece of work".— *W. E. Heitland in A Few Words on verse translation.*

"On the whole, perhaps, the best and most successful translation of a classic that exists in the English language."
—*H. A. J. Munro.*

EVERYMAN'S LIBRARY. Works. Dent, 1908. (N.Y., Dutton.)

>*Contents :*—The Odes and Epodes, by John Marshall; the Art of poetry, by the Earl of Roscommon (1680); and, Satires, by Christopher Smart (1756).

FANSHAWE (SIR RICHARD) Select poems. London, 1652.

FRANCIS (PHILIP) Works. (1742.) Repr. London, 1827.

>The Epistles and the Art of Poetry will be found in the *Chandos Classics* edition noted above.

**HOWES (FRANCIS) The Epodes, Satires and Epistles, trans. into verse. London, 1845.

>"The easy and felicitous flow of Howes is something quite above the ordinary level of English verse technique. . . . The book seems to have fallen flat . . . I came upon it through the admiration expressed by Dr. Kennedy and John Mayor, scholars keenly alive to literary merit. As a rendering of Horatian matter in Horatian manner I am not sure that it does not deserve to rank first".—*W. E. Heitland in A Few Words on verse translation.*

JONSON (BEN) The Art of poetry (1640). Reprinted, Scholartis Press, 1928.

>Of interest chiefly because of the eminence of the translator, for the version is rather rough and jerky. See also under Blakeney, above.

*JOURDAIN (M.) Translations of the odes of Horace, collected and arranged. *Temple Classics.* Dent. (N.Y., Dutton.)

> A very good selection of felicitous renderings drawn from writers of all ages—Dryden, Evelyn, W. E. Gladstone, Creech, Fanshawe, etc.

LATHAM (F. L.) Odes. Smith Elder, 1911.

> "Contains many happy renderings of Horace's prettiest epigrams and will be welcomed by all good Horatians."— *Year's Work in Class. Studies,* 1911.

LOEB CLASSICAL LIBRARY. Works: a prose translation. 2 vols. Heinemann, 1914–26. (N.Y., Putnam.)

> *Contents :*—Odes and Epodes, by Stephen Bennett; Epistles, Ars poetica, and Satires, by H. R. Fairclough.

LONSDALE (JAMES) and SAMUEL LEE. Works: a prose translation, with intro., running analysis, notes, index. *Globe Edition.* Macmillan, 1874.

*MACNAGHTEN (HUGH) The Odes: done into English verse. C.U.P., 1927. (N.Y., Macmillan.)

> This is a fine piece of work, comparable to the same translator's Catullus.

MARRIS (SIR W. S.) Odes: books 1–4; and the Saecular hymn. Frowde, 1912

*MARTIN (SIR THEODORE) Works: a verse translation. Blackwood, 1888. (N.Y., Lippincott; and, Scribner.)

> "Since Horace, by common consent, is untranslatable, the translations of him, as might be expected, are in-

numerable. On the whole, perhaps, the English reader who will study the commentary and version of Sir Theodore Martin, will get some definite idea of one of the most interesting figures in the whole range of letters, of the most modern and most familiar of the ancients."— *Frederic Harrison, in The Choice of Books.*

WICKHAM (E. C.) Horace for English readers: a trans. of the poems into English prose. O.U.P., 1903.

> SUMMARY.—The two anthologies of Horatian translations, Jourdain's and that in the *Chandos Classics* are well-nigh indispensable. They are a constant source of joy; then the reader might well concentrate on Conington, Mac-Naghten and Martin. If he cares for a prose translation the *Loeb* version will not disappoint him.

## HROSWITHA

*See* Roswitha.

## HUSS, JOHN
### (b. A.D. 1369)

SCHAFF (DAVID S.) The Church (De ecclesia): trans. with notes and intro. Allen and Unwin, 1915. (N.Y., Scribner.)

## INGULPH
### (d. A.D. 1109)

RILEY (H. T.) Chronicles of the Abbey of Croyland, with the continuation of Peter of Blois. *Bohn's Lib.* Bell, 1848.

[ 222 ]

# JACOBUS DE VITRIACO

(d. A.D. 1240).

STEWART (AUBREY) History of Jerusalem, A.D. 1180. Palestine Pilgrim's Text Soc., 1896.


# JACOBUS DE VORAGINE

(Archbishop of Genoa. 1230–1298)

CAXTON (WILLIAM) The Golden legend: lives of the Saints. (1483). Repr. Kelmscott Press, 1892; and a selection, ed. by G. V. O'Neill. C.U.P., 1914 (N.Y., Macmillan); also a reprint in 7 volumes, edited by F. S. Ellis, *Temple Classics*. Dent, 1900. (N.Y., Dutton.)


# JEROME, SAINT

(Hieronymus. 340–420)

FREMANTLE (W. H.) Principal works. *Lib. of Nicene and Post-Nicene Fathers, Second Series*. Clark, 1893. (N.Y., Scribner.)

*See* Apostolic Fathers (Appendix).


# JOCELYN

(Monk of Furness. Fl. A.D. 1200)

FORBES (A. P). The Lives of St. Kentigern. *Historians of Scotland Series, Vol. 5*. Edinburgh, 1874.

SWIFT (E. L.) The Life and acts of St. Patrick. Dublin, 1809.

# JOCELIN OF BRAKELOND

### (Fl. A.D. 1200-1210)

CLARKE (SIR E.) Chronicle. Murray, 1907.

JANE (L. C.) Chronicle. *Mediaeval Library*. Chatto and Windus, 1925. (N.Y., The Oxford Press, 1922.)

> The above translations are both good and reliable. T. E. Tomlins's "Monastic and social life of the 12th century as exemplified in the Chronicle of Jocelin of Brakelond" (Whitaker, 1844) also contains a version, but according to Sir E. Clarke, than whom there is no greater authority on the work, Tomlins had no special knowledge of his subject, and as a consequence his version contains errors, "both of omission and commission".

# JOHANNES SECUNDUS

### (1511-1536)

KELLY (W. K.) The Kisses: literally trans., with poetical versions by Nott, George Ogle and Thomas Stanley. *Bohn's Class. Lib.* Bell, 1854.

> Bound with the volume which also contains the works of Propertius, Petronius, etc. Thomas Stanley's "elegant" poetical version was reprinted in a limited edition by the Fortune Press, 1926.

*WRIGHT (F.A.) The Love-poems of Joannes Secundus: a revised Latin text, with an English verse translation. Routledge, 1929. (N.Y., Dutton.)

# JOHN OF FORDUN

### (d. A.D. 1384)

SKENE (F. J. H.) Chronicle of the Scottish nation. *Historians of Scotland Series*. Edinburgh, 1872.

# JOHN OF SALISBURY
## (1115-1180)

DICKINSON (JOHN) Policraticus: a trans. of Books 4-6, and Selections from Books 7 and 8. Knopf, 1927. (N.Y., Knopf.)

# JORNANDES
## (or Jordanes. Fl. 6th cent. A.D.)

MIEROW (C. C.) Gothic history: trans. with notes. Princeton Univ. Press, 1915.

# JULIUS CAPITOLINUS
## See Capitolinus.

# JUSTINIAN
## (Flavius Justinianus, 483-563)

ABDY (J. T.) and B. WALKER. Institutes. C.U.P., 1876. (N.Y., Macmillan.)

MONRO (C. H.) The Digest of Justinian. C.U.P., 1904. (N.Y., Macmillan.)

MOYLE (J. B.) Institutes. O.U.P., 1889; 1913.

SANDARS (T. C.) Institutes: Latin text, with trans., notes and intro. Longmans, 1898. (N.Y., Longmans.)

# JUSTINUS

## (Date uncertain)

GOLDING (ARTHUR) The Abridgement of the histories of Trogus Pompeius. London, 1563.

HOLLAND (PHILEMON) Abridgement of the histories of Trogus Pompeius. London, 1606.

WATSON (J. S.) Justin, Cornelius Nepos and Eutropius: literally trans. with notes. Bell, 1853.


# JUVENAL

## (D. Junius Juvenalis. Fl. A.D. 100)

CHAPMAN (GEORGE) Fifth satire. (1629.) Repr. in Chapman's "Minor poems and translations". Chatto and Windus, 1904, and in all editions of Chapman's poetical works.

*DRYDEN (JOHN) Satires of Juvenal and Persius. (1693.) Repr. O.U.P., edition.

> Of Juvenal, Dryden did numbers 1, 3, 6, 10, 16; of Persius, numbers 1–6.
> "The general character of this translation will be given when it is said to preserve the wit, but to want the dignity of the original."—*Dr. Johnson.*
> The vigour of this translation is such that the general reader and the scholar may both enjoy reading it, although the latter may also criticize in terms as strong as those of Dr. Johnson.

\*\*GIFFORD (WILLIAM) Satires: a verse trans. (1802.) Repr. *Bohn's Class. Lib.* Bell, 1852. (N.Y., Putnam.)

> By general consent Gifford's translation of the "Satires" is vigorous and scholarly. Many are of opinion that in those satires which Dryden translated he immeasurably surpassed Gifford. Contemporary opinion of Gifford's translation was that it was a work of extraordinary merit.

OWEN (S. G.) Satires: a prose trans. O.U.P., 1924.

\*RAMSAY (G. G.) Satires: a prose trans. *Loeb Class. Lib.* Heinemann, 1918. (N.Y., Putnam.)

STRONG (H. A.) and A. LEEPER. Satires: a verse trans. Macmillan, 1882. Rev. 1912.

> Considered to be an accurate and fair modern version.
>
> SUMMARY.—Dr. Johnson's paraphrase of the 3rd and 6th Satires will be found in "The Vanity of human wishes". Of the verse translations noted above, Dryden's and Gifford's are by far the best.

## JUNIUS BRUTUS

*See* "Vindiciae contra tyrannos".

## KIRCHMEYER, THOMAS
### (1511–1563)

GOOGE (BARNABE) The Popish kingdom; or, The Reign of Antichrist. (The Spiritual husbandrie) from Regnum Papistiarum of Naogeorgus or Kirchmeyer. (1570.) Repr., ed. by R. C. Hope. Satchell, London, 1880.

# KOMENIUS

*See* Comenius.


# KRÄMER, HENRY

(Fl. A.D. 1480)

SUMMERS (MONTAGUE) Malleus maleficarum. Rodker, 1928.

> First published at Cologne in 1489, this work has never before been translated into English.


# LACTANTIUS FIRMIANUS

(Fl. A.D. 300)

FLETCHER (W.) Works. 2 vols. *Lib. of Ante-Nicene Fathers.* Clark, 1871. (N.Y., Scribner.)


# LAMPRIDIUS, AELIUS

(Fl. 4th cent. A.D.)

Lives, *see* "Scriptores Historiae Augustae"—Appendix.


# LANGUET, HUBERT

(1518–1581)

*Supposed author* of "Vindiciae contra tyrannos", *q.v.*

# LEIBNITZ, BARON GOTTFRIED VON
## (1646–1716)

CHILD (J. M.) Early mathematical MSS. With critical and historical notes. London and Chicago, Open Court Publ. Co., 1920.

DUNCAN (G. M.) Philosophical works. (New Haven, Tuttle, 1890.)

LANGLEY (A. G.) New Essays concerning human understanding. Macmillan, 1896; and London and Chicago, Open Court Publ. Co., 1916.

**LATTA (ROBERT) Monadology and other philosophic writings. O.U.P., 1898 and 1925.

> The standard edition.

*MONTGOMERY (G. R.) Discourse on metaphysics, correspondence with Arnauld, and Monadology. London and Chicago, Open Court. Publ. Co., 1902.

> Contains the most important of the works omitted by Latta.

RUSSELL (C. W.) A System of theology. London, 1850.


# LEO I, POPE
## (Leo "The Great". d. A.D. 461)

BLAKENEY (E. H.) The Tome of Pope Leo I: Latin text, with trans., intro., and notes. S.P.C.K , 1923.

Bright (W.) Eighteen sermons on the Incarnation trans. with notes. London, 1885.

Feltoe (C. L.) Letters and sermons. *Lib. of Nicene and Post-Nicene Fathers, Second Series, Vol.* 12. Clark, 1896. (N.Y., Scribner.)

See Apostolic Fathers (Appendix).

# LEO OF ASSISI
### (? d. A.D. 1270)

La Warr (Constance, Countess de) The Mirror of perfection: being a record of St. Francis of Assisi, ascribed to his companion, Brother Leo of Assisi. Burns and Oates, 1902.

# LINNAEUS, SIR CHARLES
### (Karl von Linné. 1707–1778)

Botanical Society of Lichfield. A System of vegetables. 2 vols. Lichfield, 1783.

Kerr (R.) The Animal kingdom; or, Zoological system. London, 1792.

Smith (J. E.) A Dissertation on the sexes of plants. London, 1786.

Turton (William) A General system of nature, through the three grand kingdoms of animals, vegetables and minerals. 7 vols. London, 1802.

# LIPSIUS JUSTUS
### (1547–1606)

ANDERTON (BASIL) De Constantia: an interlude in Book II: trans. as "A Stoic in his garden" in "Sketches from a library window". Cambridge, Heffer, 1922.

LODGE (THOMAS) Life of Seneca. (1614.) Repr. *Temple Classics*. Dent, 1899. (N.Y., Dutton.)


# LIUDPRAND
### (Bishop of Cremona. 920–972)

WRIGHT (F. A.) The Works of Liudprand of Cremona (Antapodosis; Liber de rebus gestis Ottonis; Relatio de legatione Constantinopolitana.) Trans. for the first time into English, with an intro. *Broadway Mediaeval Library*. Routledge, 1930. (N.Y., Dutton.)


# LIVY
### (T. Livius. 59 B.C.–A.D. 17)

*CHURCH (A. J.) and W. J. BRODRIBB. Livy: Books XXI to XXV, The Second Punic War. Macmillan, 1853.

A reliable and standard version.

*FOSTER (B. O.) The History of Rome. 13 vols. *Loeb Class. Lib*. Heinemann, 1919. (N.Y., Putnam.) *In progress*.

HOLLAND (PHILEMON) Roman history. London, 1600.

> "If he [that is, Holland] seldom echoed the sound of
> Greek and Latin, he never missed the sense, nor did he
> fear a comparison of his own work with the classical
> texts . . . and if he did not accurately represent in English
> the prose of Livy and Plutarch, of Suetonius and Pliny,
> he left us a set of variations upon ancient motives to
> which we may listen with an independent and unalloyed
> pleasure."—*C. Whibley, Camb. Hist. Eng. Lit.*, Vol. 4,
> *pp.* 13–15.

ROBERTS (W. M.) History of Rome. 5 vols. *Everyman's
Library*. Dent, 1912–24. (N.Y., Dutton.)

SPILLAN (D.) and others. History of Rome: a literal
trans. *Bohn's Class Lib*. 4 vols. Bell, 1870–77.
(N.Y., McKay.)

# LUCAN
### (M. Annæus Lucanus. 39–65)

**DUFF (J. D.) The Civil War [Pharsalia]: a prose
translation. *Loeb Class. Lib.* Heinemann, 1928.
(N.Y., Putnam.)

GORGES (SIR ARTHUR) Pharsalia. London, 1614.

MARLOWE (CHRISTOPHER) First book of the civill warr
betwixt Pompey and Caesar: trans. line for line.
(1600.) Repr. O.U.P. edn. of Works, 1925, and
in all complete editions.

> "Marlowe tackled his difficult enterprise with fire and
> spirit. . . . There are those who find Marlowe's version
> too slow and dignified, but not content to tell the story

in his own tongue, he did his best to represent the sound and fashion of the original. . . . A bold attempt to transmute the close, congested Latin into English, not as a scholar, but as a poet might translate it."—*C. Whibley, Literary studies, p.* 90.

MAY (THOMAS) Pharsalia. London, 1627.

"Though replete with the quaint expressions peculiar to the early part of the seventeenth century, has the merit of adhering closely to the original, and is remarkable for its accuracy."—*H. T. Riley in preface to Bohn's edition.*

*RIDLEY (SIR EDWARD) Pharsalia: trans. into blank verse. Longmans, 1896. Repr. Humphreys, 1925.

"Though high praise cannot be awarded this translation, we may still be glad that it has been executed."—*Class. Rev., Vol. II, p.* 272.

RILEY (H. T.) Pharsalia: literally trans. into English prose. *Bohn's Class. Lib.* Bell, 1853.

*ROWE (NICHOLAS) Pharsalia. London, 1718 and 1722. Repr. in Chalmers's "Poets of Great Britain", vol. xx, 1820.

"The version of Lucan is one of the greatest productions of English poetry, for there is perhaps none that so completely exhibits the genius and spirit of the original."—*Dr. Johnson, Lives of the poets.*

# LUCILIUS, GAIUS
### (b. 148 B.C.)

EVANS (L.) Fragments: a literal prose trans. *Bohn's Class. Lib.* Bell, 1848.

# LUCILIUS JUNIOR

*See* Aetna, The.


# LUCRETIUS

(T. Lucretius Carus. 99–55 B.C.)

ALLISON (SIR ROBERT) On the nature of things: a trans. into English verse. Humphreys, 1919.

> "It has real vigour and vitality. If the spirit of the poet is lacking, the spirit of the man is there . . . and in many of the great passages of the poem, such as the end of the first book, Sir Robert rises to great heights."— *C. Bailey, Class. Rev., Vol. 34.*


BAILEY (C.) On the nature of things: a prose trans. O.U.P., 1910.

> This is an admirable version.


BUSBY (THOMAS) On the nature of things: a verse translation. London, 1813.

> A fair rendering in monotonous heroic couplets.


CREECH (THOMAS) On the nature of things: a verse trans. Oxford, 1682. Repr. in Anderson's "Poets of Great Britain", Vol. xiii, 1793.

> "Not without merit, but though there is some masculine writing in it, there is little grace or beauty, and a good deal of triviality and vulgarity."—*J. Conington, Miscellaneous writings, Vol. I, p. 250.*

DRYDEN (JOHN) On the nature of things: a verse trans.
(1692.) Repr. in O.U.P. edn., and in all complete
editions.

> Dryden did parts only of books 1, 2, 3 and 5.
> "A translation in a style that has no note of either the
> vigour or the music of its original."—*Lord Morley in
> Recollections, Vol.* 2, *p.* 121.

EVELYN (JOHN) An Essay on the first book of Lucretius,
with a metrical version and notes. London, 1656.

JACKSON (THOMAS) On the nature of things: a prose
translation. Oxford, Blackwell, 1929.

> An interesting version in rhythmical iambic prose.

*LEONARD (W. E.) On the nature of things: a metrical
version. *Everyman's Library.* Dent, 1921. (N.Y.,
Dutton.)

MALLOCK (W. H.) On life and death (from "On the
nature of things"). Black, 1900. (Portland, Mosher,
1919.)

> In the metre of FitzGerald's "Omar Kháyyám".

**MUNRO (H. A. J.) On the nature of things: a prose
translation. (1864.) Repr. *Popular Lib.* Bell, 1914.
(N.Y., Harcourt.)

> The best version, and not likely to be surpassed.
> "It is not only a most faithful literal rendering of the
> original, but a remarkable literary achievement. . . .
> Munro's edition, and still more his translation, are not
> superseded, and it is probable that they never can be.
> For power of thought, united with power of style, will
> secure the permanence of his work."—*J. D. Duff in
> preface to Bell's reprint.*

[ 235 ]

ROUSE (W. H. D.) On the nature of things: a prose trans. *Loeb Class. Lib.* Heinemann, 1924. (N.Y., Putnam.)

> SUMMARY.—Up to the present time the best versions of Lucretius have been in prose, and of these, Munro's is by common consent by far the best; but something, of course, of the poetic power of the philosopher is lost. Mallock and Leonard are both readable and are recommended by scholars.

## MANILIUS, M.
### (Fl. *c*. A.D. 25)

CREECH (THOMAS) The Five books of Manilius: a verse trans. London, 1697.

> It is commonly thought that this version was not by Creech. Some say it is the work of Sir Edward Sherborne, but the matter remains a question of doubt.

## MAP, WALTER
### (1137–1209)

JAMES (M. R.) De Nugis curialium: trans. with notes, ed. by E. S. Hartland. *The Cymmrodorion Record Series.* London, 1923.

*TUPPER (FREDERICK) and M. B. OGLE. De Nugis curialium(Of courtiers' trifles). Chatto and Windus, 1924. (N.Y., Macmillan.)

## MARCELLINUS

*See* Ammianus Marcellinus.

# MARTIAL

(M. Valerius Martialis. 38–104)

*BOHN (H. G.) Epigrams: complete literal trans., each with one or more verse trans. *Bohn's Class. Lib.* Bell, 1877.

> "This translation is unusually good."—*Barrett Wendell in The Traditions of European Literature.*

COURTHOPE (W. T.) Martial: selections trans. or imitated in English verse. Murray, 1914.

*FRANCIS (A. L.) and H. F. TATUM. Selected epigrams. C.U.P., 1923. (N.Y., Macmillan.)

> *See* note under Pott and Wright.

KER (W. C.) Epigrams: a prose version. 2 vols. *Loeb Class. Lib.* Heinemann, 1919–1920. (N.Y., Putnam.)

NIXON (PAUL) A Roman wit: epigrams of Martial, rendered into English [verse.] (Boston, Houghton, 1921.)

**POTT (J. A.) and F. A. WRIGHT. Twelve books of epigrams: a verse trans. *Broadway Trans.* Routledge, 1923. (N.Y., Dutton.)

> "The version of Messrs. Francis and Tatum is the work of sound scholars, has the advantage of brief notes, and is sometimes, perhaps generally, the more literal; it would be strange if it did not succeed occasionally where the other fails. But Messrs. Pott and Wright are the cleverer; they command a far larger variety of metrical

devices—roundels, triolets, even the FitzGerald stanza—
and a livelier lot of rhymes; they are smarter in bringing
out points. Anyone interested in Martial is strongly
recommended to acquire both renderings. In IX. xcvii,
such a challenge to a translator, I should not have thought
that either Messrs. Francis and Tatum's method or their
climax could have been bettered, had I not turned to the
new *Broadway* version."—*A. Y. Campbell in London
Mercury, Vol.* 12, *p.* 330.

# MATTHEW OF WESTMINSTER
## (Fl. A.D. 1200)

YONGE (C. D.) Flowers of history, especially such as
relate to the affairs of Britain. 2 vols. *Bohn's Lib.*
Bell, 1853.

> According to Sir Frederic Madden, the greater portion
> of this work is an abridgment of Matthew Paris's
> Chronicle, *q.v.*, probably prepared under Paris's direction.

# MELA, POMPONIUS
## (Fl. A.D. 40)

GOLDING (ARTHUR) De Situ orbis. London, 1590.

# MILTON, JOHN
## (1608–1674)

BEGLEY (WALTER) Nova Solyma, the ideal city; or,
Jerusalem regained: an anonymous romance
written in the time of Charles I, and attributed to
John Milton, with intro., trans., etc. (1648.)
Murray, 1902.

[ 238 ]

COWPER (WILLIAM) Milton's Latin poems trans. into English verse. (1792.) Repr. O.U.P. edition of Cowper's poetical works, etc.

HUNT (LEIGH) Milton's Latin poems: a selection trans. into English verse. (1823.) Repr. O.U.P. edition of Hunt's poetical works, 1923, etc.

SUMNER (CHARLES) Prose works, including the Christian Doctrine: trans. and edited. 5 vols. *Bohn's Lib.* Bell. (N.Y., Macmillan.)

## MINUCIUS FELIX
### (Fl. A.D. 200)

\*BRODRIB (A. A.) The Octavius. Bell, 1903.

> "It is not often that one meets with a translation from an ancient author that is so satisfactory as Brodrib's."— *R. C. Seaton, Class. Rev., Vol.* 18.

FREESE (J. H.) The Octavius. *Ante-Nicene Christian Lib.* Clark, 1898. (N.Y., Scribner.)

## MONUMENTUM ANCYRANUM
*See* "Res Gestae divi Augustae" (Greek Section—Appendix).

## MORE, SIR THOMAS
### (1478–1535)

RICHARDS (G. C.) Utopia: trans. into modern English Blackwell, 1923.

> "The translation is very well done."—*London Mercury.*

Robynson (Ralph) Utopia. (1551.) Repr. *Bohn's Lib.*, Bell (N.Y., Harcourt.); and in *The Scott Lib.*, together with Roper's "Life of More" (Scott. Publ. Co.); and by the O.U.P., edited with the text of 1518, with intro., notes, etc. by J. H. Lupton, 1895.

## MORNAY, DUPLESSIS

*Supposed author of* "Vindiciae contra tyrannos", *q.v.*

## MOSHEIM, JOHANNES LORENZO VON
### (1694–1755)

Maclaine (A.) Ecclesiastical history. (1765.) Repr. 6 vols. London, 1825.

*Murdock (J.) Institutes of ecclesiastical history, ancient and modern: a literal trans. 3 vols. (1832.) Repr. edited by W. Stubbs, 3 vols. (Longmans, 1863); and revised by H. L. Hastings. 3 vols. Boston, Mass., 1892.

## NAEVIUS, GNAEUS
### (270–199 B.C.)

Merry (W. W.) Selections, in "Fragments of Roman poetry" O.U.P., 1891.

## NAOGEORGUS
*See* Kirchmeyer, Thomas.

# NAMATIANUS, C. RUTILIUS

*See* Rutilius.


# NENNIUS

(Fl. A.D. 810)

GILES (J. A.) History of the Britons, in "Six Old English chronicles". *Bohn's Lib.* Bell, 1848.


# NEPOS, CORNELIUS

(100–25 B.C.)

*ROLFE (J. C.) Works: the text, with an English translation. *Loeb Class. Lib.* Heinemann, 1929. (N.Y., Putnam.)

WARD (GEORGE) A Close trans. of the lives of Miltiades and Epaminondas. 16 pp. Holland and Co., London, 1901.

WATSON (J. S.) Works: literally trans. in "Justin, Eutropius and Cornelius Nepos". *Bohn's Lib.* Bell, 1876.


# NEWTON, SIR ISAAC

(1642–1727)

MOTTE (ANDREW) Mathematical principles of natural philosophy, to which is added, a System of the world. (London, 1803.) (Repr. "Principia, . . With a life by N. W. Chittenden". N.Y., 1848.)

# NOVA SOLYMA

*See under* Milton, John.


# NOVATIAN

(Fl. A.D. 250)

MOORE (HERBERT) On the Trinity. S.P.C.K., 1919.
(N.Y., Macmillan.)

*See also* Apostolic Fathers (Appendix).


# ORDERICUS VITALIS

(1075–1143)

FORESTER (T.) Ecclesiastical history of England and
Normandy. 4 vols. *Bohn's Lib.* Bell. 1855. (N.Y.,
Macmillan.)


# ORIGEN

(186–254)

BELLAMY (JAMES) Against Celsus. London, 1660.

CHAUCER (GEOFFREY) The Complaynt of Mary Mag-
dalene in the "Boke of fame". (1526.) Repr.
O.U.P. edition, 1906; etc.

CROMBIE (F.) Writings. 13 vols. *Ante-Nicene Library.*
Clark, 1869–72. (N.Y., Scribner.)

# OROSIUS

THORPE (B.) Literal English trans. of King Alfred's Anglo-Saxon version of the "Compendious history of the world" by Orosius. *Bohn's Lib.* Bell, 1853.

# OTTO I

(Bishop of Freising. 1114–1158.)

MIEROW (CHARLES C.) The two cities (Historia de duabus civitatibus): a chronicle of universal history to the year A.D. 1146. Trans. with intro. and notes. O.U.P., 1930. (N.Y., Columbia Univ. Pr., 1928.)

# OVID

(P. Ovidius Naso. 43 B.C.–A.D. 18)

*LOEB CLASSICAL LIBRARY. The Works of Ovid: a prose translation. 5 vols. Heinemann, 1926. (N.Y., Putnam.) *In progress.*

> *Contents :*—The Fasti, by Sir J. G. Frazer; The Metamorphoses, by F. J. Miller, 2 vols.; The Tristia and Ex Ponto, by A. L. Wheeler; The Herodies and Amores, by Grant Showerman.
>
> Of Miller's version of the "Metamorphoses" E. H. Alton wrote: "I fear that these two volumes will not win much commendation. The translation is at times creditable, even excellent, but readers will be annoyed continually by blunders and slipshod paraphrase."—*Class. Rev.*, Vol. 30, *p.* 238.

RILEY (H. T.) Complete works: a literal translation into English prose, with notes. 3 vols. *Bohn's Class. Lib.* Bell, 1869. (N.Y., McKay.)

> This is one of the more successful literal versions of ancient authors in the famous Bohn's library. Although, as one would expect, the translation reads heavily at times on account of its literalness, yet on the whole the volumes may all be read with interest.

## The Art of Love

DRYDEN (JOHN) The Art of Love: a verse translation of Book I; and, Three Epistles. (1680.) Repr. in the Oxford and all other complete editions of Dryden.

> Dryden left vigorous renderings of Book 1 of the "Metamorphoses", and parts of Books 8–15. Book 12 is translated in its entirety. From the "Art of Love" he did Elegies 1 and 4 from Book 1, and 19 from Book 2.

*MAY (LEWIS) The Art of love: a prose translation. Lane, 1926.

WRIGHT (F. A.) The Art of love: a verse translation under the title of "The Lover's Handbook". *Broadway Trans.* Routledge, 1920. (N.Y., Dutton.)

## The Metamorphoses

CAXTON (WILLIAM) Metamorphoses, Books x–xv, now for the first time printed from the MS. in the Pepysian Library, Cambridge. Edited by S. Gaselee and H. F. Brett-Smith. Oxford, Blackwell, 1925.

GARTH (SIR SAMUEL) Metamorphoses (1717.) Repr. frequently, and notably in Chalmers's "Poets of Great Britain", vol. xx, 1810.

> The two volumes issued by Valpy in 1833 form a very good edition in which to become acquainted with the best of the eighteenth-century translations of the "Metamorphoses" and the "Epistles". Garth, Dryden, Pope and Congreve and Addison all contributed to the work, which, although unequal, as might well be expected from such a composite edition, yet contains parts which have yet to be excelled.

GOLDING (ARTHUR) The Metamorphoses: a verse translation. (1565–7.) Repr. under the title of "Shakespeare's Ovid", edited by W. H. D. Rouse. *King's Library*. Dent, 1904. (N.Y., Dutton.)

> "The chief characteristic of the translation is its evenness. It never falls below, or rises above, a certain level. Turn whichever page you choose, and you will come upon lines unhampered by the Latin original. . . . The craftsmanship is neither slovenly nor distinguished. . . . The style is rapid, fluent and monotonous. The author is never a poet and never a shirk. You may read his mellifluous lines with something of the same simple pleasure which the original gives you. Puttenham paid him no more than his due when he described him as 'in translation very cleare and very faithfully answering his author's intent'."
> —*Charles Whibley, Camb. Hist. Eng. Lit., Vol. 4, p. 20.*

## Miscellaneous Works

CHAPMAN (GEORGE) The Banquet of sense: a verse translation. (1595.) Repr. frequently, and notably in "Minor Poems and Translations", Chatto and Windus, 1904.

**\*\*Frazer (Sir James George)** The Fasti: Text, translation and commentary. 5 vols. Macmillan, 1929. (N.Y., Macmillan.)

> This work includes the Latin text, an English prose translation, exegetical commentary, indices, plans and illustrations. The text has been revised with the help of photographs of six of the principal manuscripts now in Rome, Paris, Brussels, Munich and Oxford. The Commentary deals fully with the matter of the Fasti, attempting to elucidate all historical, mythical and religious allusions.

**Marlowe (Christopher)** Elegies. Repr. *Haslewood Books*. Etchells and Macdonald, 1925, and frequently in other editions of Marlowe's works, also notably in the Oxford Univ. Press edition, 1925.

> "Judged by absolute standards . . . must be agreed to be a failure both as poetry and as a rendering of the Latin. . . . The translator has manifestly been supported by a real poetical fervour. Occasionally the lines have a very melodious cadence . . ."—*C. F. Tucker Brooke, in the O.U.P. edition.*

# OWEN, JOHN
## (1560–1622)

**Cowper (William)** Epigrams: trans. into English verse. (1790.) Repr. in all complete editions of Cowper's poems, and notably in the Oxford Univ. Press edition.

**Harvey (Thomas)** Latine epigrams: a verse translation. London, 1677.

# PALLADIUS, RUTILIUS TAURUS AEMILIANUS

### (Fl. A.D. 350)

ANONYMOUS. On hosbondrie. Edited from the unique MS. of *c.* 1420 in Colchester Castle, by B. Lodge. (With a rhyme index edited by S. J. H. Herrtage.) 2 vols. E.E.T.S., London, 1873–9.

OWEN (THOMAS) The Fourteen books on agriculture. London, 1807.

# PARIS, MATTHEW

### (Fl. *c.* A.D. 1200)

GILES (J. A.) Chronica majora, 1235–1273. 3 vols. *Bohn's Class. Lib.* Bell, 1852. (N. Y., Macmillan.)

See also *under* Matthew of Westminster.

# PATERCULUS, C. VELLEIUS

### (*c.* 19 B.C.–A.D. 31)

SHIPLEY (F. W.) Compendium of the history of Rome. *Loeb Class. Lib.* Heinemann, 1924. (N.Y., Putnam.)

Included in the volume entitled "Res Gestae divi Augustae".

WATSON (J. S.) Compendium of the history of Rome: a literal trans. *Bohn's Class. Lib.* Bell, 1876.

Included in the volume containing the works of Sallust and Florus.

# PATRICK, SAINT

## (c. 372–463)

WHITE (NEWPORT) The Writings and life. *Trans. of Christian Lit. Series.* S.P.C.K., 1920. (N.Y., Macmillan.)

WHITE (W. J. D.) Libri sancti Patricii: the Latin writings of St. Patrick, ed. with intro., trans. and notes. Royal Irish Academy, 1905.

WRIGHT (C. H. H.) Writings: trans. with notes. *Christian Classics.* R.T.S., 1889.


# PERSIUS FLACCUS, A.

## (34–62)

\*\*CONINGTON (J.) The Satires, with a trans. and commentary. Rev. by H. Nettleship. O.U.P., 1893.

> This prose translation is recommended as "by far the best existing version of Persius" by *G. G. Ramsay in the Preface to the Loeb edition.*

DRYDEN (JOHN) The Satires: a verse trans. (1693.) Repr. O.U.P. edition. Anderson's "Poets of Great Britain", 1793; Chalmers's "English poets", 1810, etc.

\*GIFFORD (WILLIAM) The Satires. (1817.) Repr. *Bohn's Class. Lib.* Bell, 1852. (N.Y., Harcourt.)

HEMPHILL (SAMUEL) Satires Bell, 1901. (N.Y., Harcourt.)

> "The translation is smooth, and generally clear and accurate."—*Class. Rev., Vol.* 15, *p.* 426.

RAMSAY (G. G.) The Satires: a prose version. *Loeb Class. Lib.* Heinemann, 1918. (N.Y., Putnam.)

> Included in the volume which also contains the "Satires" of Juvenal.

## PERVIGILIUM VENERIS
### *See* Catullus.

## PETER MARTYR ANGLERIUS
### (1459–1525)

EDEN (RICHARD) The Decades of the New World or West India. (1555.) Repr. Birmingham, 1885.

LOK (M.) History of the West Indies. (1612.) Repr. in Hakluyt's "Collection of early voyages", Vol. 5. London, 1809.

MACNUTT (F. A.) De Orbo Novo: the eight decades of Peter Martyr of Anghera. 3 vols. Putnam, 1912. (N.Y., Putnam.)

## PETER OF BLOIS
### (*c.* 1135–1204)

RILEY (H. T.) Ingulph's Chronicles of the Abbey of Croyland, with a continuation by Peter of Blois. *Bohn's Class. Lib.* Bell, 1848.

# PETRARCHA, FRANCESCO
## (1304–1374)

COSENZA (M. E.) Letters to classical authors, trans. with a comm. Univ. Chicago Press, 1910.

DRAPER (WILLIAM H.) Petrarch's secret; or, The Soul's conflict with passion: three dialogues between himself and St. Augustine. Chatto and Windus, 1911.

ROBINSON (J. H.) and H. W. ROLFE. Petrarch: the first modern scholar. . . .: selections from correspondence with Boccaccio and other friends, with intro. and notes. (1898.) Rev., Putnam, 1914. (N.Y., Putnam.)

TILDEN (FRANK WM.) On the contemplative life: trans. with notes and essay. *Indiana Univ. Studies.* Bloomington (Ind.), 1922.

TWYNE (THOMAS) Phisicke against fortune as well prosperous as adverse, conteyned in two books. London, 1579.


# PETRONIUS ARBITER, T.
## (Fl. A.D. 60)

### *Bellum Civile*

BALDWIN (FLORENCE T.) Bellum civile: edited with intro. and comm., and a blank verse translation. Frowde, 1911.

"As for the translation, it is not inspired, but it gives the sense."—*Stephen Gaselee, Class. Rev., Vol. 26, p. 65.*

FANSHAWE (SIR RICHARD) Bellum civile: a verse translation. 1655.

> This excellent translation is probably the first into English, and will be found in the preface to Fanshawe's translation of Camoen's "Lusiad".

## The Satyricon

**BURNABY (WILLIAM) The Satyricon. (1694.) Repr. with intro. by C. K. Scott-Moncrieff. *Abbey Classics*. Chapman and Dodd, 1923. (Boston, Small.)

> "He is not always scholarly, but he uses an excellent colloquial English with a common-sense interpretation, which carries him over the many gaps in the story without any palpable difference in texture."—*C. K. Scott-Moncrieff*.

FIREBAUGH (W. C.) The Satyricon: a complete and unexpurgated translation. 2 vols. *Privately printed*. (N.Y., Boni and Liveright, 1922.) Another edition adapted and revised was published by Longmans, 1927.

**HESELTINE (MICHAEL) The Satyricon. *Loeb Class. Lib*. Heinemann, 1913. (N.Y., Putnam.)

> "I should myself be inclined to say that it is the best translation that I know of an ancient author. Every page is full of clever and telling phrases, and the whole is so wonderfully natural and spirited that one marvels how so much vitality can go hand in hand with such close and excellent scholarship."—*H. Garrod, Class. Rev., Vol.* 28, *p.* 203.

KELLY (W. K.) The Satyricon. *Bohn's Class. Lib*. Bell, 1854.

> A good version, but now out of print.

LOWE (W. D.) Cena Trimalchionis: edited with notes and a trans. Bell, 1905.

> A version of the most famous episode in the "Satyricon".

MITCHELL (J. M.) The Satyricon. *Broadway Trans.* Routledge, 1923. (N.Y., Dutton.)

> The translator has not rendered the grosser parts, but, following the example of the majority of *Loeb* translators, has left them in the original Latin. This is a distinct loss with an author such as Petronius.
>
> SUMMARY.—There is a good, racy version by Jack Lindsay, published in London by the Fanfrolico Press, but this is practically unobtainable now, except at a very enhanced price. For the ordinary reader, the choice lies between Burnaby's manly version and Heseltine's.

# PHAEDRUS
### (Fl. A.D. 15)

RILEY (H. T.) Fables, with a metrical version by Christopher Smart. *Bohn's Class. Lib.* Bell, 1853.

> This translation is bound with the comedies of Terence. Some of Smart's verse translations will also be found in volume 2 of Howe and Harrer's *Spirit of the Classics*, Harper, 1924.

# PHILO JUDAEUS
### (20 B.C.–A.D. 40)

COLSON (F. H.) and G. H. WHITAKER. Works. 10 vols. *Loeb Class. Lib.* Heinemann, 1929. (N.Y., Putnam.) *In progress.*

JAMES (M. R.) Biblical antiquities. *Trans. of Early Documents.* S.P.C.K., 1917. (N.Y., Macmillan.)

TILDEN (F. W.) On the contemplative life: a trans. with notes and an essay. (Indiana Univ. Studies.) 1922.

YONGE (C. D.) Works. *Bohn's Eccles. Lib.* Bell, 1854. (N.Y., Harcourt.)

# PIUS II
(Aeneas Sylvius Piccolomini. 1405–1464)

ALLEN (CHARLES) The Historie of Eurialus and Lucretia. London, 1639.

BARCLAY (ALEXANDER) Three eclogues of the miseries and manners of the Count and Countess. London, 1570.

*GRIERSON (FLORA) The Tale of two lovers. Constable, 1929.

> A new translation of *De Duobus Amantibus*. The tale was very popular in the seventeenth century and was translated under such various titles as are noted above.

# PLAUTUS, T. MACCIUS
(254–184 B.C.)

ALLISON (SIR R.) Comedies: a verse trans. A. L. Humphreys, 1914.

HYDE (R. W.) and E. C. WEIST. The Menaechmei: trans. into English verse and prose. O.U.P., 1930. (Harvard U.P.)

**NIXON (PAUL) Comedies: a prose trans. 2 vols. *Loeb Class. Lib.* Heinemann, 1916–1925. (N.Y., Putnam.)

> "He not only commands an idiomatic and nervous style of English, but he has hit the right tone, and in difficult passages he shows that he has studied Plautus as a scholar."—*Class. Rev.*

RILEY (H. T.) Comedies: a literal prose trans. 2 vols. *Bohn's Class. Lib.* Bell, 1852.

ROGERS (B. B.) Menaechmei: a verse trans. Bell, 1908.

THORNTON (BONNEL) Comedies: a blank verse trans. 5 vols. London, 1769–1774.

> "As a poetical work it is impossible to speak of it in other than terms of admiration; but from the circumstance of its being in blank verse it is not sufficiently close to convey to the English reader an accurate idea of the peculiar style of the author."—*H. T. Riley in the Bohn edition.*

WRIGHT (F. A.) and H. L. ROGERS. Plautus: a verse trans. of three comedies (Rudens, Aulularia, Pseudolus). *Broadway Trans.* Routledge, 1924. (N.Y., Dutton.)

# PLINY THE ELDER

(C. Plinius Secundus. 23–79)

BAILEY (KENNETH C.) Chapters on chemical subjects. Part 1. Edit. with trans., and notes. Arnold, 1929.

> The first translation of any part of the "Natural History" since the *Bohn* edition of 1855 noted below.

BOSTOCK (JOHN) and H. T. RILEY. Natural history. 6 vols. *Bohn's Class. Lib.* Bell, 1855.

**HOLLAND (PHILEMON) Natural history of the world. London, 1601.

> "In some respects his 'Pliny' is Holland's masterpiece. . . . Few writers have ever kept so consistently at a high level of excellence."—*Charles Whibley, Camb. Hist. Eng. Lit., vol. 4.*

JEX-BLAKE (K.) Chapters on the history of art. Macmillan, 1896.

# PLINY THE YOUNGER
## (C. Plinius Caecilius Secundus. 62-114)

FIRTH (J. B.) Letters. 2 vols. *Scott Lib.* Walter Scott, 1910–16.

LEWIS (J. D.) The Letters of the younger Pliny: a literal trans. Kegan Paul, 1879.

**MELMOTH (WILLIAM) Letters. (1746.) Repr. rev. by Bosanquet. *Bohn's Class. Lib.* Bell, 1878, and by W. L. Hutchinson. 2 vols. *Loeb Class. Lib.* Heinemann, 1923. ( N.Y., Putnam.)

> "Melmoth's translation of Pliny's letters, published in 1746, not only delighted contemporary critics—amongst whom Warton pronounced it a better work than the original—but deservedly ranks as a minor English classic. Apart from its literary excellence, it has the supreme

merit of reflecting the spirit of the original, and that to a degree now unattainable. . . . No modern rendering can capture the ease and felicity of Melmoth's; for they came of his living in a world like Pliny's own. . . . Judged even by the easy canons of his time in regard to translation his work is extraordinarily loose and inaccurate; a good deal of it is simply paraphrase, and in many cases the sense is flagrantly wrong."—*W. L. Hutchinson in the Loeb introduction.*

J. W. Duff writes of the *Loeb* edition: "Standing alone, it [i.e. Melmoth's original translation] could be read as a minor English classic, but facing the original . . . it would, if unrevised, have shown to great disadvantage. Skill and taste characterize the alterations."—*Class. Rev., Vol.* 30, *p.* 200.


# POLLIO, TREBELLIUS

*See* Trebellius Pollio.


# PROPERTIUS, SEXTUS

(50–16 B.C.)

*BUTLER (H. E.) Elegies: a prose trans. *Loeb Class. Lib.* Heinemann, 1912 (N.Y., Putnam.)

GANTILLON (P. J. F.) Elegies: a literal trans. ed. by W. K. Kelly with poetical versions by Elton and Nott. *Bohn's Class. Lib.* Bell, 1854.

**PHILLIMORE (J. S.) Works: a prose trans. O.U.P., 1906.

# PRUDENTIUS CLEMENS, AURELIUS

(b. A.D. 348)

POPE (R. MARTIN) and R. F. DAVIS. Cathemerinon; or, Hymns: the text with a verse trans. *Temple Classics*. Dent, 1900. (N.Y., Dutton.)

THACKERAY (F. ST. JOHN) A Selection from the works of Prudentius: rendered into English verse. Bell, 1890.

# PUBLILIUS SYRUS

(Fl. 43 B.C.)

JOHNSON (SAMUEL) Choice sentences. London, 1776.

RUSSEL (GEORGE) Sentences. Cork, 1769.

# QUINTILIAN

(M. Fabius Quintilianus. 35–100)

**BUTLER (H. E.) Works. 4 vols. *Loeb Class. Lib.* Heinemann, 1927. (N.Y., Putnam.)

GUTHRIE (WILLIAM) Institutes of eloquence. 2 vols. (1756.) Repr. London, 1805.

WATSON (J. S.) Institutes of oratory: a literal trans. 2 vols. *Bohn's Class. Lib.* Bell, 1856.

# "RES GESTAE DIVI AUGUSTAE"

*See* Greek Section (Appendix).


# RICHARD OF BURY

(Richard Aungerville. 1281–1345)

THOMAS (E. C.) Philobiblon. (1888.) Repr. *Mediaeval Lib.* Chatto and Windus, 1925.

"A monumental achievement and the only trustworthy rendering."—*Sir Israel Gollanz, Preface.*


# RICHARD OF CIRENCESTER

(1335–1401)

GILES (J. A.) The Ancient state of Britain. In "Six Old English chronicles". *Bohn's Lib.* Bell, 1848.


# RICHARD OF DEVIZES

(Fl. A.D. 1190)

GILES (J. A.) Chronicles of the Crusades. *Bohn's Lib.* Bell, 1841.

Included in the volume which contains the chronicles of Geoffrey De Vinsauf.


# ROGER OF HOVEDEN

(d. *c.* A.D. 1201)

RILEY (H. T.) Annals of English History, 732–1201. 2 vols. *Bohn's Lib.* Bell, 1853.

# ROGER OF WENDOVER

## (d. A.D. 1236)

GILES (J. A ) Flowers of history. *Bohn's Lib*. Bell, 1849.


# ROLLE, RICHARD, OF HAMPOLE

## (1290–1349)

MISYN (RICHARD) Incendium amoris; and, De Emendatione vitae. (1435.) Repr. E.E.T.S., 1896, and Edited and done into modern English by F. M. M. Comper. Methuen, 1920. (Another edition, N.Y., Benziger.)


# ROSWITHA

## (932–1002)

ST. JOHN (CHRISTOPHER) Plays. *Mediaeval Lib*. Chatto and Windus, 1923. (N.Y., Oxford Press.)


# RUFINUS, TYRANNIUS

## (345–410)

MORRISON (E. F.) Commentary on the Apostles' Creed. Methuen, 1916.

WHITAKER (CHARLES) Commentary on the Apostles' Creed. Bell, 1908. (N.Y., Macmillan.)

*See also* Apostolic Fathers (Appendix).

# RUTILIUS NAMATIANUS, CLAUDIUS

## (Fl. A.D. 413)

SAVAGE-ARMSTRONG (G. F.) De Reditu suo libri duo: a verse trans. Edited with notes by C. H. Keene. Bell, 1907. (N.Y., Macmillan.)

# SACCHERI, GIROLAMO

## (b. A.D. 1667)

HALSTEAD (G. B.) Euclides vindicatus. Edited with Latin text and trans. London and Chicago, Open Court Publ. Co., 1920.

# SALLUST

## (C. Sallustius Crispus. 86–35 B.C.)

HEYWOOD (THOMAS) The Two most worthy and notable histories, viz. The Conspiracie of Catiline and The Warre which Jugurth for many years maintained. (1608.) Repr. *Tudor Trans.* Constable, 1924. (N.Y., Knopf.)

> "He turned Sallust into the speech of his own day, following the example of his predecessors."—*C. Whibley in the preface to the 1924 reprint.*

MAIR (JOHN) Catiline's conspiracy. Edinburgh, 1741.

POLLARD (A. W.) The Catiline and the Jugurtha. Macmillan, 1882.

\*ROLFE (J. C.) Works. *Loeb Class. Lib.* Heinemann, 1920. (N.Y., Putnam.)

> "A readable and straightforward translation—somewhat undistinguished. . . . The English is clear and correct and the translation accurate."—*H. E. Butler, Class. Rev., Vol.* 35.

ROSE (WILLIAM) History of Catiline's conspiracy and the Jugurthine War. London, 1751.

> "A very faithful, accurate and excellent version."— *Lowndes's Bibliographer's Manual.*

WATSON (J. S.) Works. In "Florus and Velleius Paterculus". *Bohn's Class. Lib.* Bell, 1861.

# SALVIANUS MASSILIENSIS

## (Fl. A.D. 450)

ANONYMOUS. A Second and third blast of retrait from plaies and theaters: the one thereof was sounded by Salvain, a reverend bishop long since dead, (in the sixth book of "De gubernatione dei"), the other by a worshipful gentleman now alive, set forth by Anglo-Phile Eutheo. (1580.) Repr., edited by W. C. Haslett. *Roxburghe Lib.* 1868.

"R. T." A Treatise of God's government and of the justice of His present dispensations in this world. Trans. by R. T., Presbyter of the Church of England. Pref. by Mr. Wagstaffe. London, 1700.

# SELDEN, JOHN

## (1584–1654)

OGG (DAVID) Ad fletam dissertatio: a parallel trans. with intro. and notes. C.U.P., 1925. (N.Y., Macmillan.)


# SENECA

### (M. Annaeus Seneca, *The Elder*. d. A.D. 39)

EDWARDS (W. A.) The Suasoriae. Intro., essay, text, translation and notes. C.U.P., 1928. (N.Y., Macmillan.)


# SENECA

### (L. Annaeus Seneca, *The Younger*)

### (4 B.C.–A.D. 65)

LOEB CLASSICAL LIBRARY. Works. 7 vols. Heinemann, 1917. (N.Y., Putnam.) *In progress.*

*Contents:*—Moral essays, by J. W. Basores; Epistulae morales, by R. M. Gummere (3 vols.); Tragedies, a prose translation by F. J. Miller (2 vols.); and Apocolocyntosis, by W. H. D. Rouse, in Petronius' "Satyricon" in the same series; F. J. Miller's translation of the Tragedies is also published in London by Fisher Unwin (1907) and in the U.S.A. by the Univ. of Chicago Press. "This translation above all else is eminently readable. . . . In general Mr. Miller is exceedingly faithful to his original."—*Class. Rev., Vol.* 22, *p.* 191.

## On Benefits

GOLDING (ARTHUR) On benefits. London, 1578.

LODGE (THOMAS) On benefits. (1614.) Repr., with life
by Justus Lipsius, edit. by W. H. D. Rouse.
*Temple Classics.* Dent, 1899. (N.Y., Dutton.)

> "Thomas Lodge in 1614 published his monumental
> version of Seneca's prose, a work undimmed by com-
> parison even with Holland's translation of Plutarch's
> 'Morals' (1603)."—*Charles Whibley, in Camb. Hist. Eng.
> Lit., Vol. 4.*

STEWART (A.) On Benefits; minor dialogues together
with the dialogue on clemency. *Bohn's Class. Lib.*
Bell, 1859.

## The Letters

LODGE (THOMAS) Letters. (1614.) Repr. in "Selections
from Seneca's prose, trans. by L'Estrange and
Lodge", edited by Walter Clode. *Camelot Series.*
Walter Scott, 1888.

SUMMERS (W. C.) Select letters. Macmillan, 1910.

## Tragedies

BRADSHAW (WATSON) Ten tragedies: a prose trans
Allen and Unwin, 1902.

HARRIS (ELLA) Tragedies: a verse trans. O.U.P., 1904.

NEWTON, THOMAS, *Editor.* Seneca: his tenne tragedies.
(1581.) Repr. with an introduction by T. S. Eliot.
2 vols. *Tudor Translations Series.* Constable, 1927.

STUDLEY (JOHN) The Eyght tragedie, entituled "Agamemnon". (1566.) Repr. (with "Medea"), edit.
by E. M. Spearing. D. Nutt, 1913.

> "Studley's 'Agamemnon' deserves peculiar notice both
> as a specimen of one of the earliest efforts at translation
> by our native writers and for the ability with which it
> was performed."—*British Bibliography, Vol. 2, pp.* 372–77.

## Miscellaneous Works

CLARKE (JOHN) Physical science in the time of Nero: a
trans. of the "Quaestiones naturales" of Seneca;
with notes by Sir A. Geikie. Macmillan, 1910.
(N.Y., Macmillan.)

> This is considered an excellent translation.

LANGSDORF (W. B.) On tranquillity of mind and
providence. Putnam, 1900.

L'ESTRANGE (SIR ROGER) Morals. (1678.) Repr. *Camelot
Series*. Walter Scott, 1888.

> An abstract from Seneca's work, translated very loosely.

# SIDONIUS APOLLINARIS

(C. Sollius Apollinaris Sidonius. 430–483)

DALTON (O. M.) LETTERS. 2 vols. O.U.P., 1925.

> This translation is the first yet attempted in English.

# SILIUS ITALICUS, C.
## (25–101)

Ross (T.) The Second Punic War between Hannibal and the Romanes: the whole 17 books Englished from the Latine . . . with a continuation from the triumph of Scipio to the death of Hannibal; a verse trans. London, 1661–72.

> A part of this work is given in lengthy quotation in Howe and Harrer's "Spirit of the Classics", vol 2. (Harper, 1924.)

Tytler (H. W.) Punics: trans. in heroic couplets. London, 1828.

# SIMEON OF DURHAM
## (Fl. A.D. 1129)

Stevenson (J.) Historical works. London, 1870.

# SOLINUS, JULIUS
## (Fl. A.D. 250)

Golding (Arthur) Works. London, 1587.

# SPARTIANUS, AELIUS
## (c. A.D. 300)

Maude (W.) De die natale: "The Natal day by Censorinus"; and, The Life of the emperor Hadrian by A. Spartianus. Camb. Ency. Co., N.Y., 1900.

*See also* "Scriptores historiae Augustae" (Appendix).

# SPINOZA, BENEDICT DE
### (1632–1677)

BOYLE (A.) Ethics and De Intellectus emendatione. *Everyman's Library*. Dent, 1910. (N.Y., Dutton.)

ELWES (R. H. W.) Chief works. 2 vols. *Bohn's Lib*. Bell, 1883.

MACCALL (W.) Tractatus politicus. London, 1854.

**WHITE (W. H.) Ethics demonstrated in geometrical order. Rev. by A. M. Stirling. Duckworth, 1894. Rev. Frowde, 1910. (N.Y., Oxford Press.)
  Considered the best English translation.

**—— Tractatus de intellectus emendatione. Duckworth, 1899.

WOLF (A.) Tractatus de deo et homine. Black, 1910.

# STATIUS, P. PAPINIUS
### (45–96)

LEWIS (WM. L.) The Thebaid: trans. into English verse, with notes. London, 1773. Repr. in Chalmers's "Poets of Great Britain", Vol. xx, 1820.

*MOZLEY (J. H.) Works: the Latin text with a prose translation. 2 vols. *Loeb Class. Lib*. Heinemann, 1928. (N.Y., Putnam.)

POPE (ALEXANDER) The First book of the Thebaid.
(1703.) Repr. in Elwyn and Courthope's ed. of
Pope's works, 1871; and by O.U.P., etc.

SLATER (D. A.) Silvae: trans. with notes. O.U.P.,
1908.

## STRADA, FAMIANUS
### (1572–1647)

LANCASTER (THOMAS) The Siege of Antwerp. London,
1655.

STAPYLTON (SIR ROBERT) Of the Low Country Warres.
London, 1650.

## SUETONIUS
### (C. Suetonius Tranquillus. A.D. 75–160)

**HOLLAND (PHILEMON) History of the twelve Caesars,
Emperors of Rome. (1606.) Repr. *Tudor Trans.*,
ed. by C. Whibley, Nutt, 1899; and *Broadway
Trans.*, ed. by J. H. Freese, Routledge, 1924. (N.Y.,
Dutton.)

> "If he [i.e. Holland] seldom echoed the sound of Greek
> and Latin he never missed the sense. . . . Excellent in
> tone and movement as is the Suetonius, in some respects
> his Pliny is Holland's masterpiece."—*C. Whibley, Camb.
> Hist. Eng. Lit., Vol. 4.*

ROLFE (J. C.) Works. 2 vols. *Loeb Class. Lib.* Heinemann, 1914. (N.Y., Putnam.)

> "The translation does not lack the qualities of vigour and lightness: on the contrary, it is decidedly readable; but it is disappointing that the editor of a classic should suffer from defective proof-reading, inaccuracies in translation, and neglect of sound English." [Then follows more than three columns of suggested errors, inaccuracies, etc., which will probably be corrected in later editions.]— *J. Wight Duff, Class. Rev., Vol.* 30, *p.* 167.

# SULPICIA

### (Fl. A.D. 100)

EVANS (L.) Satires: a literal prose trans. In "The Satires of Juvenal, Persius, etc.". *Bohn's Class. Lib.* Bell, 1877.

GRAINGER (J.) Poems: a verse trans. (*c.* 1760.) Repr. Chalmers's "English Poets", 1810.

# SULPICIUS SEVERUS

*See* Apostolic Fathers (Appendix).

# SWEDENBORG, EMANUEL

### (1688–1772)

ACTON (ALFRED) The Animal Kingdom considered anatomically, physically and philosophically. (Phil., Boericke.)

BAYLEY (F.) Divine love and wisdom. *Everyman's Lib.*
Dent, 1909. (N.Y., Dutton.)

—— Divine Providence. *Everyman's Lib.* Dent, 1909.
(N.Y., Dutton.)

SWEDENBORG SOCIETY. Works: trans. from the Latin.
London, 1870– (N.Y., Amer. Swedenborg Publishing Co.)

> The enormous number of books written by Swedenborg
> have nearly all been translated during the last fifty years,
> and have been issued by this society, from whom they
> may be obtained.

# SYMPOSIUS

(Caelius Firmianus Symposius. Date uncertain)

DU BOIS (ELIZABETH HICKMAN) The Hundred riddles
of Symphosius: trans. into English verse with the
text, intro. and notes. Woodstock, Vermont, Elm
Tree Press, 1912.

# SYRUS

*See* Publilius Syrus.

# TACITUS, P. CORNELIUS

(b. A.D. 50)

CHURCH (A. J.) and W. J. BRODRIBB. Annals: a literal
trans. Macmillan, 1891.

CHURCH (A. J.) and W. J. BRODRIBB. The Agricola, Germany and the Dialogue on Oratory: trans. with notes and a map. Macmillan, 1893.

—— The History: trans. with notes and a map. Macmillan, 1894.

> "A scholarly version, faithful to the original, and pure in its English."—*The Athenæum.*

FYFE (W. HAMILTON) Histories. O.U.P., 1912.

> A correct version in good English.

—— The Agricola, Germania and Dialogues. O.U.P., 1908.

LOEB CLASSICAL LIBRARY. Works. 4 vols. Heinemann, 1925. (N.Y., Putnam.)

> *Contents :*—The Dialogues, by Sir William Peterson, and Agricola and Germania, by Maurice Hutton; The Histories, by Clifford H. Moore (2 vols.); The Annals, by John Jackson.

*MURPHY (ARTHUR) The Histories, the Germania and the Agricola. 5 vols. (1793.) Repr. London, 1830; and *Everyman's Library*, 2 vols., Dent, 1908. (N.Y., Dutton.)

> "Alone of the older translations has achieved some sort of permanence."

*RAMSAY (SIR G. G.) The Histories. Murray, 1915. (N.Y., Dutton.)

*RAMSAY (SIR G. G.) The Annals. 2 vols. Murray, 1904–1909.

> A smooth and dignified version. "May long remain the best English version of the Annals."—*Class. Rev., Vol.* 24, *p.* 19.

## TERENCE
### (P. Terentius, *Afer.* 195–159 B.C.)

COLMAN (G.) Comedies: trans. into blank verse. London, 1810.

PERRY (F.) Comedies. a verse translation. O.U.P., 1929.

—— The Phormio. O.U.P., 1929.
> Reprinted from the complete volume noted above.

RILEY (H. T.) The Comedies: literally trans. into English prose, with notes. *Bohn's Class. Lib.* Bell, 1883.

*RITCHIE (W.) Plays: trans. into parallel English metres. Bell, 1927.

*SARGEAUNT (JOHN) Works: a prose version. 2 vols. *Loeb Class. Lib.* Heinemann, 1912. (N.Y., Putnam.)

## TERTULLIAN
### (Q. Septimius Florens Tertullianus. 164–240)

BINDLEY (T. HERBERT) On the testimony of the soul and on the "Prescription" of heretics. *Early Church Classics.* S.P.C.K., 1914. (N.Y., Macmillan.)

DODGSON (C.) Works. 2 vols. *Lib. of the Fathers*. J. and
  J. H. Parker. Oxford, 1842.

*SOUTER (ALEXANDER) Works. S.P.C.K., 1919. (N.Y.,
  Macmillan.)

—— Apology. C.U.P., 1917. (N.Y., Macmillan.)

> "Professor Souter's translation is admirable. The frequent
> tendency to paraphrase is an indication of the difficulty
> of translation, but easy flowing English is not sacrificed."
> —*Class. Rev., Vol.* 32, *p.* 128.

*THELWALL (S.) and others. Works. 3 vols. *Ante-
  Nicene Lib*. Clark, 1867——. (N.Y., Scribner.)

# THOMAS AQUINAS, SAINT
## (1226–1274)

DOMINICAN FATHERS, *Editors*. Summa theologica. 21
  vols. Burns and Oates, 1922.

# THOMAS OF ECCLESTON
## (Fl. A.D. 1270)

CUTHBERT (*Father*) The Friars and how they came to
  England: a trans. of "De Adventu F. F. Minorum
  in Angliam". Thomas Baker, 1903; 1909.

SALTER (E. GURNEY) The Coming of the Friars to
  England and Germany: The Chronicles of Thomas
  of Eccleston and Jordan of Giano. Dent, 1926.
  (N.Y., Dutton.)

# THOMAS OF MONMOUTH

## (Fl. A.D. 1150)

JESSOP (AUGUSTUS) and M. R. JAMES. Life and miracles of St. William of Norwich, now first edited from the unique manuscript, with intro., trans. and notes. C.U.P., 1896. (N.Y., Macmillan.)


# THOU, JACQUES A. DE

## (known as J. A. Thuanus. 1553–1617)

WILSON (B.) History of his own time, 1543–1607: books 1 to 6 only. 2 vols. London, 1729.


# TIBULLUS, ALBIUS

## (55–19 B.C.)

CRANSTOUN (J.) Elegies: a verse translation. Edinburgh, 1872.

GRAINGER (JAMES) Works: a verse translation. (1759.) Repr. in Chalmers's "English Poets", vol. 20, 1810; and in the *Bohn's Class. Lib.* Bell, 1854.

KELLY (W. K.) Erotica: the poems of Catullus and Tibullus, etc.: a literal prose translation, with the metrical versions of Lamb and Grainger. *Bohn's Class. Lib.* Bell, 1854.

**\*\*POSTGATE (J. P.) Works: a prose translation.** *Loeb Class. Lib.* Heinemann, 1912. (N.Y., Putnam.)

> Included in the volume which also contains Cornish's translation of Catullus.
> Postgate's translation of Tibullus "can be read right through, and enjoyed like a new and beautiful thing existing for itself. . . . The very finest shades of the original are reflected in his version. . . . Throughout whole elegies the mind is kept entranced by the translator's word-craft and his fine sense for the poet's thought. This Englishing of Tibullus must be the best thing of its kind produced for many years."—*J. F. Roxburgh, Class. Rev., Vol.* 28, *p.* 139.

**\*WILLIAMS (T. C.) Poems. Boston, 1905.**

# TREBELLIUS POLLIO
### (Fl. A.D. 306)

Lives. *See* "Scriptores Historiae Augustae" (Appendix).

# TRISMEGISTUS, HERMES

*See* Hermes, in Greek Section.

# TROGUS POMPEIUS
### (Fl. A.D. 10)

**CODRINGTON (ROBERT) The History. London, 1654.**

**GOLDING (ARTHUR) The Abridgment of the histories. London, 1564.**

WATSON (J. S.) Justin's history of the world, extracted from Trogus Pompeius, Cornelius Nepos and Eutropius: a literal trans. *Bohn's Class. Lib.* Bell, 1876. (N.Y., Macmillan.)

## ULPIANUS, DOMITIUS
### (170–228)

ABDY (J. T.) and B. WALKER. Commentaries of Gaius and the Rules of Ulpian. O.U.P., 1885.

## VALERIUS FLACCUS
*See* Flaccus, Valerius.

## VALERIUS MAXIMUS
### (Fl. A.D. 29)

SPEED (S.) A View of the religion, laws, and dispositions of the Romans. London, 1678.

## VALLA, LAURENTIUS
### (1407–1457)

COLEMAN (C. B.) The Treatise on the Donation of Constantine. Yale Univ. Press, 1922.

> "The translation is written in excellent English, and retains the spirit of the original."—*A. C. Clark, Class. Rev., Vol.* 38, *p.* 88.

# VARRO, M. TERENTIUS
### (116–27 B.C.)

HARRISON (FAIRFAX) "A Virginia Farmer." Cato's treatise on farm management, with Varro's treatise. Macmillan, 1913. (N.Y., Macmillan.)

STORR-BEST (LLOYD) On farming: trans. with an intro. and commentary. *Bohn's Class. Lib.* Bell, 1912.

> "The translation is a good and interesting one."—*W. Warde Fowler, Class. Rev., Vol.* 27, *p.* 105.

# VEGETIUS RENATUS, FLAVIUS
### (Fl. A.D. 386)

CLARKE (JOHN) Military institutions. London, 1767.

SADLER (JOHN) The Foure bookes of Flavius Vegetius Renatus briefelie contayninge a plaine forme, and perfect knowledge of Martiall policye feates of chivalrie and whatsoever pertayneth to warre. London, 1572.

# VELLEIUS PATERCULUS
### *See* Paterculus.

# VINCENT OF LERINS, SAINT
### (d. A.D. 450)

BINDLEY (T. H.) Commonitorium. *Early Church Classics.* S.P.C.K., 1914. (N.Y., Macmillan.)

Heurtley (*Canon*) Commonitorium. *Nicene and Ante-Nicene Fathers, Second Series.* Clark, 1895. (N.Y., Scribner.)

> *See* Apostolic Fathers (Appendix).


# "VINDICIAE CONTRA TYRANNOS"

Anonymous. Vindiciae contra tyrannos: a defence of liberty against tyrants; or, Of the lawful power of the prince over the people and of the people over the prince. Written in Latin and French by Junius Brutus. Edited by H. J. Laski. Bell, 1924. (N.Y., Harcourt.)

> The probable author of this work was either Duplessis Mornay, a minister of Henri IV, or Hubert Languet, 1518–1581. It was translated in order to influence English public opinion on the Civil War.


# VIRGIL

### (P. Vergilius Maro. 70–19 B.C.)

**Dryden (John) The Works of Virgil: a trans. into heroic couplets. (1697.) Repr. O.U.P., *Chandos Classics*, Warne, etc.

> Pope characterized this most famous version as "the most noble and spirited translation that I know in any language", while Dr. Johnson said that "it satisfied his friends and silenced his enemies". The following may be taken as typical of the modern critic's attitude: "England, we think, is to be congratulated on the posses-

sion of one really fine poem, not more unlike Virgil than its rivals in external feature, while possessing to an infinitely greater degree than any of them that 'energy divine' which constitutes the essence of all poetry, ancient or modern . . . we may congratulate ourselves on the possession of a splendid English epic, in which most of the thoughts are Virgil's, and most of the language Dryden's."—*J. Conington, Miscellaneous Writings, Vol.* 1, *p.* 181.

FAIRCLOUGH (H. R.) Works: a prose trans. 2 vols. *Loeb Class. Lib.* Heinemann, 1916. (N.Y., Putnam.)

LONSDALE (J.) and S. LEE. Works: a prose trans. *Globe Ed.* Macmillan, 1871. (N.Y., Macmillan.)

**RHOADES (JAMES) The Poems of Virgil: a blank verse translation. *World's Classics.* O.U.P., 1907.

Considered by Professor Postgate and other eminent scholars to be one of the most successful renderings of Virgil yet made. "By common consent this is an admirable translation of Virgil, perhaps the best in existence." —*Class. Rev., Vol.* 22, *p.* 256.

## The Aeneid

BALLARD (HARLAN HOGE) The Aeneid. (1902.) Repr. 1908, 1911 and 1930. (N.Y., Scribner.)

A successful rendering in hexameters. This version has been found to be particularly valuable when introducing Virgil to children. Lacking something of the grandeur of the classic translations, it yet combines faithfulness and ease to such a degree as to make it worthy of a wider public in England, where it is little known. Its great merit is in its "readableness".

Billson (C. J.) The Aeneid: text, with a blank verse trans. Blackwell, 1906. (N.Y., Appleton, 1924.)

> "A version of more than average merit, highest in the most elevated passages, but not sufficiently sustained throughout."—*J. P. Postgate, Class. Rev., Vol. 20, p. 362.*

*Conington (J.) The Aeneid: a verse trans. Longmans, 1870. (N.Y., Scott, 1916; Burt; and McKay.)

—— Poems; and a prose version of the Aeneid. In Vol. 2 of "Miscellaneous writings". Longmans, 1872.

> Of the verse translation of the Aeneid: "Undoubtedly takes its place henceforward as by far the most poetical as it is also the most faithful and scholarly rendering of the original."—*W. Lucas Collins.*
> "Professor Conington has produced a version singularly faithful (save in the point which he abandons) and pleasant and spirited withal."—*C. S. Calverley.*
> Calverley's parenthesis refers to Conington's assertion that he did not attempt "to represent the characteristic art of Virgil's language".

Fanshawe (Sir Richard) The Loves of Dido and Aeneas: the fourth book of the Aeneid. (1652.) Repr., edited with notes by A. L. Irvine. Oxford, Blackwell, 1925.

Jackson (J.) The Aeneid: a prose trans. O.U.P., 1910.

*Mackail (J. W.) The Aeneid: a prose trans. Macmillan. (1885.) 1908. (N.Y., Macmillan.)

MORRIS (WILLIAM) The Aeneid: a verse trans. Longmans, 1876.

> "His translation can be read from beginning to end with delight: it is only when it is compared with the original that it fails. His version . . . is archaistic."—*Hugh Macnaghten, National Review, Vol.* 86, *p.* 886.

**RHOADES (JAMES) The Aeneid: trans into blank verse. Longmans, 1907. For note see under first sections where the reprint is recorded.

SURREY (HENRY, EARL OF) [The Aeneid.] Certain bokes (2 and 4) of Virgiles Aeneis turned into English metre. (1557.) Repr. *Aldine Edition.* Bell, 1831; Chalmers's "English poets", 1820.

> "In his translation from the Aeneid he comes before us as the inventor of English blank verse. Having invented blank verse, Surrey used it timidly and with caution. . . . He keeps close enough to the Latin original, and for all his neatness fills his reader with wonder that so poor an instrument as he wields should have attained in the hands of Shakespeare and Milton the effect which it did of variety and pomp."—*C. Whibley, Literary Studies, p.* 89.
> "I wish with all my heart that Henry, Earl of Surrey, had finished his translation of the Aeneid; it seems to me one of the very best."—*Hugh Macnaghten, National Review, Vol.* 86, *p.* 879.

TAYLOR (E. FAIRFAX) The Aeneid: a verse trans. *Everyman's Lib.* Dent, 1907. (N.Y., Dutton.)

> A smoothly flowing translation in the Spenserian stanza.

WILLIAMS (T. C.) The Aeneid: a blank verse trans. Boston, 1908. (Harvard U.P., 1915.)

> This version is highly praised by American critics. According to Barrett Wendell, indeed, it approaches nearer to Virgil than any other English translation. It has not attracted much attention in England.

\*Bowen (Sir Charles) Eclogues: a verse trans. Murray, 1887.

> Regarded by many scholars as on the whole a very successful effort.

Burghclere (Lord) Georgics: a blank verse trans. Murray, 1904.

\*Calverley (C. S.) Eclogues: a verse trans. (1868.) Repr. bound with Theocritus in *Bohn's Popular Lib.* Bell, 1913. (N.Y., Harcourt.)

> "Not even Sir Charles Bowen has more deftly caught the spirit of the Eclogues."—*R. Y. Tyrrell, Preface to Bohn's reprint.*

Mackail (J. W.) Eclogues and Georgics. Rivingtons, 1889. Repr. Longmans, 1914. (N.Y., Longmans.)

Royds (T. F.) Eclogues and Georgics: a verse trans. *Everyman's Lib.* Dent, 1907; rev. edn. Oxford, Blackwell, 1922.

> Summary.—The basis of any approach to Virgil in English may well be Dryden's translation. Of the modern versions of the "Aeneid", Conington's and Rhoades's are indispensable. The most successful versions of the "Eclogues" are Bowen's and Calverley's.

# VITRINGA

### (Campegius Vitringa or Vitruga. 1659–1722)

Bernard (J. L.) The Elder, the Synagogue and the Church. London, 1842.

# VITRUVIUS POLLIO
### (Fl. 13 B.C.)

GWILT (J.) Architecture. London, 1825.

MORGAN (MORRIS H.) and A. A. HOWARD. Ten books
   on architecture (ascribed to Vitruvius Pollio).
   C.U.P., 1914. (Harvard Univ. Press.)


# VIVES, JUAN LUIS
### (1492–1540)

SALTER (F. R.) De subventione pauperum: trans. for
   the first time into English in "Some early tracts
   on poor relief". Methuen, 1926.

SHERWOOD (M. M.) Concerning the relief of the poor:
   a letter addressed to the Senate of Bruges, 1526.
   (N.Y., School of Social Work, 1917.)

WATSON (FOSTER) On Education: a trans. of "De
   tradendis disciplinis". C.U.P., 1913. (N.Y., Macmillan.)

—— Tudor Schoolboy life: the Dialogues (Linguae
   Latinae Exercitatio), trans. for first time. Dent,
   1908. (N.Y., Dutton.)


# VOPISCUS, FLAVIUS
### (Fl. A.D. 290)

Lives. *See* "Scriptores historiae Augustae" (Appendix).

# VORAGINE, JACOBUS DE

*See* Jacobus de Voragine.


# VULCACIUS, GALLICANUS

Lives. *See* "Scriptores historiae Augustae" (Appendix).


# WILLIAM OF MALMESBURY

### (1095–1143)

SHARPE (J.) Chronicles. Edited by J. A. GILES. *Bohn's Lib.* Bell, 1847.

# MISCELLANEOUS COLLECTIONS

ALDINGTON (RICHARD) Latin poems of the Renaissance. 2 vols. Egoist Press, 1919.

BLAKENEY (E. H.) *Editor*. Hymns of the Western Church. Partridge, 1930.

> Contains the Latin text with the best translations available. Many of Neale's fine renderings are included.

HOWE (GEORGE) and G. A. HARRER. The Spirit of the classics. 2 vols. Vol. 1: Roman literature in translations. (N.Y., Harper, 1927.)

> An admirable survey, invaluable to the general reader. Translations are given of selections from the greatest writers and from many minor authors. The latter include Cato, Aulus Gellius, Phaedrus, Persius, Silvius Italicus, Valerius Flaccus, etc.

MAGIE (D.) Scriptores historiae Augustae. 3 vols. *Loeb Class. Lib.* Heinemann, 1923. (N.Y., Putnam.)

> Contains the lives of Hadrian, Aelius, Marcus Aurelius and other Emperors from A.D. 117–284 by Aelius Spartianus, Julius Capitolinus, Vulcacius Gallicanus, Aelius Lampridius, Trebellius Pollio, and Vopiscus.

MAXWELL (SIR HERBERT) The Chronicle of Lanercost: trans. with notes. Maclehose, 1913.

> May be regarded as a continuation of the annals of Roger of Hoveden.

STEBBING (WILLIAM) Some masterpieces of Latin poetry thought into English Verse. Unwin, 1920.

STEBBING (WILLIAM) Greek and Latin anthology thought into English verse. 3 vols. Unwin, 1923.

SYMONDS (J. A.) Wine, women and song: the Mediaeval Latin students' songs; trans. into English verse, with an essay. Chatto and Windus, 1907. (N.Y., Oxford Press.)

WADDELL (HELEN) The Wandering scholars. Constable, 1927. (Boston, Houghton.)

> This book contains numerous translations of famous mediaeval songs. The skill and scholarship of these versions have been almost universally praised by scholars and literary critics.

—— Mediæval Latin Lyrics. Constable, 1929.

> The publication of this volume revealed to a wide public the hitherto unsuspected beauties of many of the fugitive songs of the mediaeval troubadour. The translations maintain a very high level and may be read with delight by both scholar and general reader.

# APPENDIX

# THE WRITINGS OF THE APOSTOLIC FATHERS

LAKE (KIRSOPP) The Apostolic Fathers. 2 vols. *Loeb Class. Lib.* Heinemann, 1912. (N.Y., Putnam.)

> *Contents :*—The Epistles of Clement, Ignatius and St. Polycarp; The Didache; or Teaching of the Twelve Apostles; The Epistle of Barnabus; The Shepherd of Hermas; The Martyrdom of St. Polycarp, by the Church of Smyrna; The Epistle to Diognetus.
>
> "An admirable rendering in terse, modern English."— *Class. Rev., Vol.* 27, *p.* 200.

LIGHTFOOT (J. B.) The Apostolic Fathers: revised texts, with notes, dissertations and translations. 6 vols. Macmillan, 1890.

> *Contents :*—St. Clement of Rome; St. Ignatius; St. Polycarp; The Epistle of Barnabas; Hermes.

PUSEY (E. B.) *Editor.* A Library of the Fathers of the Holy Catholic Church, anterior to the Division of the East and West. Trans. by Members of the English Church. 50 vols. Parker, Oxford, 1842.

> *Contents :*—St. Ambrose; St. Athanasius; St. Augustine; St. Chrysostom; St. Justin Martyr; St. Cyril; St. Cyprian; St. Irenaeus; Tertullian; St. Gregory.

*ROBERTS (A.) and J. DONALDSON. The Writings of the Apostolic Fathers prior to A.D. 325. 24 vols. *Ante-Nicene Christian Library.* Edinburgh, Clark, 1867–1872. (N.Y., Scribner.)

> *Contents :*—St. Clement; St. Barnabas; St. Polycarp; The Pastor of Hermas; Justin Martyr; Athenagoras; Tatian; Theophilus; Clement of Alexandria; St. Irenaeus; Tertullianus; Hippolytus, Bishop of Rome; St. Cyprian; Origen; Novatian; Minucius Felix; Methodius; Alexander of Lycopolis; Peter of Alexandria; Victorinus and Commodianus; Gregory Thaumaturgius; Dionysius of Alexandria and Archelaus; Lactantius; Origen *contra* Celsum.

*SCHAFF (PHILIP) *Editor*. Select Library of Nicene and Post-Nicene Fathers. 2 series. 28 vols. Edinburgh, Clark, 1890–1908. (N.Y., Scribner.)

> *Contents :*—St. Augustine; St. Chrysostom; Eusebius; Socrates; Sozomenus; Theodoret; St. Jerome; Gennadius; Rufinus; St. Athanasius; St. Hilary of Poitiers; John of Damascus; St. Ambrose; St. Basil; Gregory the Great; Ephraim Syrus; Gregory Nyssa; St. Cyril of Jerusalem; St. Gregory Nazianzum; Sulpitius Severus; Vincent of Lerins; John Cassian; Leo.
>
> The two great Libraries of the Fathers noted above are the most extensive of all the collections of these writings. Formerly published in the United States by the Christian Literature Company, they are now under the imprint of Scribner.

SWAN (C.) The Gesta Romanorum (1824.) Repr. Bell, 1877, and *Broadway Trans*. Routledge, 1924. (N.Y., Dutton.)

> "Swan's translation is on the whole very faithful; where the boldness of the Latin justifies, often indeed enforces it, he amplifies the narrative judiciously, and he makes occasional omissions."—*E. A. Baker, Preface to 1924 edition.*

*WRIGHT (F. A.) The Fathers of the Church: a selection from the writings of the Latin Fathers. Routledge, 1928. (N.Y., Dutton.)

> An excellent selection for the general reader, containing an introduction, biographical notes and translations of the most important parts of the writings of Tertullian, Ambrose, Jerome, Cyprian, Arnobius and Lactantius.

# LIST OF PRINCIPAL BOOKS
## CONSULTED

Allibone (S. A.) Dictionary of Authors. Lippincott.

American Catalogue.

Amos (F. R.) Early theories of Translation. Columbia Univ. Pr., 1920.

Arnold (Matthew) On Translating Homer. Macmillan.

Bailey (C.) Legacy of Rome. O.U.P.

Bailey (John) The Continuity of Letters. O.U.P.

—— Poets and poetry. O.U.P., 1911.

Bohn (H. G.) General Catalogue of Greek and Latin Books for sale. 1850.

British Museum Catalogue.

Brueggemann (L. W.) A View of English Translations. II. 1797.

Brunet (J. C.) Manuel du Libraire. Paris, 1860.

Bywater (J.) Four Centuries of Greek Learning. O.U.P.

Cambridge History of English Literature. C.U.P.

Chambers's Biographical Dictionary.

Chapman (J. B.) Horace and his Poetry. Harrap, 1911.

Chislett (W.) Classical influence in English Literature. Boston, 1918.

Claim of Antiquity. O.U.P., 1920.

Clark (F. L.) The *Iliad* in Translation. C.U.P., 1927.

Clarke (A.) A Bibliographical Dictionary. 6 vols. 1802.

Classical Quarterly.

Classical Review.

Collins (J. Churton) Greek influence on English Literature. Pitman.

—— Illustrations of Tennyson.

Conington (J.) English Translations of Vergil. (Quarterly Review, 1861.)

—— Miscellaneous Writings. Longmans, 1872.

Courthope (W. J.) History of English Poetry. 6 vols. Macmillan.

Cox (E. M.) Poems of Sappho. Williams and Norgate.

Dixon (W. Macneile) English Epic and Heroic Poetry. Dent.

Dryden (John) Essays and Critical Writings. O.U.P.

English Catalogue of Books.

Esdaile (E. Arundell) List of English Tales and Prose Romances Printed before 1740. Bibliographical Society, 1912.

Foster (F. M. K.) English Translations from the Greek. Columbia Univ. Pr.

Goad (Caroline) Horace in the English Literature of the 18th Century. Yale Univ. Pr., 1918.

Goldmark (R. I.) Studies in the Influence of the Classics on English Literature. Columbia Univ. Pr.

Hallam (Henry) European literature.

Harris (W. J.) The First English Translations. Routledge, 1907.

Harrison (Frederic) The Choice of Books. Macmillan.

Harrison (J. S.) Platonism in English Poetry of the 16th and 17th Centuries. Columbia Univ. Pr.

Heitland (W. E.) A Few Words on Verse Translation. C.U.P., 1925.

Henderson (W. B. Drayton) Swinburne and Landor. Macmillan, 1918.

Hoffmann (S. F. W.) Bibliographisches Lexicon der gesammten Litteratur der Griechen. 1838.

Hübner (E.) Bibliographie der Klassischen Alterthumswissenschaft. 1889.

Hyde (J.) Bibliography of Works of Swedenborg.

Jebb (Sir R. C.) Growth and influence of Classical Greek poetry. Macmillan.

Jiriczek (O. L.) Specimens of Tudor Translations from the Classics. Heidelburg, 1923.

Kerlin (R. T.) Theocritus in English Literature. Yale Univ. Pr., 1910.

Kitchin (G.) Sir Roger L'Estrange. K. Paul, 1913.

Leonard (R. M.) Echoes from the Classics. O.U.P.

Lowndes (W.) Bibliographer's Manual. Bohn, 1864.

Lucas (E. L.) Seneca and Elizabethan Tragedy. Harrap, 1922.

Macnaghten (Hugh) Little Masterpieces from the Greek Anthology. Gowans and Gray, 1924.

Masqueray (Paul) Bibliographie pratique de la Littérature grecque. 1914.

Mayor (J. B.) Guide to the Choice of Classical Books. 1885.

Moss (J. W.) A Manual of Classical Bibliography. 1830.

Moulton (R. G.) Ancient Classical Drama. O.U.P., 1898.

Murray (Gilbert) Classical Tradition in Poetry. O.U.P., 1927.

Mustard (W. P.) Classical echoes in Tennyson. Columbia Univ. Pr.

Nelson's Best Books.

Newcastle-on-Tyne Public Library. Classical Catalogue. 1912.

Nitchie (Elizabeth) Vergil and the English Poets. Columbia Univ. Pr., 1918.

Palmer (H. R.) List of English Editions of Translations before 1640.

Phillimore (J. S.) Some Remarks on Translation and Translations. O.U.P., 1919.

Pope (Alexander) Preface to Homer.

Postgate (J. P.) Translations and Translation. Bell, 1922.

Saintsbury (George) Short History of English Literature. Macmillan.

—— Editor. Periods of European Literature. Blackwood.

Sandys (Sir J. E.) A History of Classical Scholarship. C.U.P.

Schweiger (F.) Handbuch der klassischen Bibliographie. 1834.

Society for the Promotion of Roman Studies. Catalogue of Books in the Library. 1924.

Spearing (E. M.) Elizabethan Translations of Seneca's Tragedies. 1912.

Stapfer (P.) Shakespeare and Classical Antiquity. 1880.

Symonds (J. A.) Studies in the Greek Poets. Black.

Thomson (J. A. K.) The Greek Tradition. Allen and Unwin, 1915.

Tolman (H. C.) The Art of Translating. Boston, 1901.

Tytler (A. F., *Lord Woodhouslee*) Essay on the Principles of Translation. *Everyman's Library*. Dent. (Reprint.)

Tucker (T. G.) The Foreign Debt of English Literature. Bell,
1907.

United States Catalogue, to date.

Warren (Sir T. H.) Essays on Poets and Poetry. Murray, 1909.

Warton (Thomas) History of English Poetry. Ward, Lock.

Wendell (Barrett) Traditions of European Literature. Murray, 1921.

Whitaker's General Catalogue of Books, to date.

Wise (B. A.) Influence of Statius on Chaucer.

Wolff (S. L.) Greek Romances in Elizabethan Prose Fiction.
Columbia Univ. Pr.

Wulf (de) History of Mediæval Philosophy. 2 vols. Longmans,
1926–7.

Year's Work in Classical Studies, to date.

# INDEX OF TRANSLATORS

[ 296 ]

[ 300 ]

[ 303 ]

[ 306 ]

PRINTED IN GREAT BRITAIN
BY UNWIN BROTHERS LIMITED
LONDON AND WOKING